Nelson

English Language Reference Book

Debbie Croft

grammar
punctuation
spelling
vocabulary
text types

Nelson English Language Reference Book Second Edition

Text: Debbie Croft
Publisher: Tania Mazzeo
Editor: Susan Keogh
Project editor: Annabel Smith
Text and cover designer: Mariana Maccarini
Typesetter: Straive
Production controller: Alice Kane

Originally published in Australia in 2010

ISBN 978 0 17 047432 0

Cengage Learning Australia
Level 5, 80 Dorcas Street
Southbank VIC 3006 Australia
Phone: 1300 790 853
Email: aust.nelsonprimary@cengage.com

For learning solutions, visit **cengage.com.au**

Printed in China by 1010 Printing International Ltd
1 2 3 4 5 6 7 27 26 25 24 23

Contents

Introduction

The ***Nelson English Language Reference Book Second Edition*** can be used to improve written and spoken communication skills. Covering the areas of grammar, punctuation, spelling, vocabulary and text types, it will support understanding of successful communication and the development of essential literacy skills.

The ***Nelson English Language Reference Book Second Edition*** has been specifically developed to assist students and teachers to understand:

- essential grammar rules at both word and sentence level
- correct use of punctuation
- spelling rules and generalisations
- the benefits of an extended vocabulary
- the structure and language features of different text types.

Structure

Each of the five chapters of the ***Nelson English Language Reference Book Second Edition*** has been colour-coded to allow students and teachers to find information quickly and easily.

Boxes throughout the ***Nelson English Language Reference Book Second Edition*** highlight additional key points and also explain important terms, which are underlined in the text. Information in these boxes reinforces and extends knowledge of specific language features.

Chapter 1 Grammar explains and provides examples of a wide selection of grammatical terms to help students and teachers apply the rules of grammar consistently.

In **Chapter 2 Punctuation**, a range of punctuation marks, which make meaning clearer, are explained. Punctuation makes texts easier to understand by breaking sentences and phrases into logical parts.

Chapter 3 Spelling provides useful strategies to learn and apply when attempting to write less familiar words correctly. These strategies are based on visual knowledge, phonological knowledge, morphemic knowledge and etymological knowledge.

Proficient spellers rely on a combination of all these different strategies to master the complexities of accurately writing with a large vocabulary of words.

The word lists in **Chapter 4 Vocabulary and Word Lists** contain useful suggestions for building vocabulary, along with lists of commonly misused words and homophones.

There are nine regular text types presented in **Chapter 5 Text Types**. Each of these contains a typical structure and some characteristic language features. Additionally, an example of a hybrid text is included, although there is a degree of variation in the structure and language features of this text type. These aspects of the hybrid text can vary depending on the text types represented and the manner in which the author chooses to present the information. Finally, a section about poetry is included because it is a common text form.

Teachers can also use the ***Nelson English Language Reference Book Second Edition*** to develop, confirm or extend students' knowledge about language. Teachers can refer to the word lists, figurative language examples, spelling generalisations and text type information during modelled writing sessions. This serves to demonstrate to students that all writers should feel comfortable to access resource material to enhance or edit their own writing. Teachers can also direct students to specific sections of the book to encourage them to take responsibility for their own learning.

The ***Nelson English Language Reference Book Second Edition*** is an up-to-date, accurate and essential resource for students and teachers, reflecting the ever-changing nature of the English language.

This reference book is also aligned to the state and national curricula. Scan the QR code or enter the short URL below to access relevant curriculum alignment charts.

clnk.au/nelrb

1 Grammar

Grammar is the set of rules used in a language. The function of grammar is to make language as clear and as logical as possible so a writer's ideas are understood by the reader. A good writer needs to have a strong understanding of how grammar works. Once a writer has achieved this, they can apply it to any writing task, with success.

Different types of words, called language features, form the basic building blocks of grammar. Language features include nouns (e.g. common nouns and collective nouns), pronouns (e.g. personal pronouns and possessive pronouns), adjectives (e.g. classifying adjectives and factual adjectives), verbs (e.g. relating verbs and sensing verbs), conjunctions, connectives and phrases.

Writers use these language features in sentences. Different types of sentences can be used to build a text, e.g. sentences that are statements, questions, commands or direct speech. Sentences are used to form paragraphs, and paragraphs are used to construct whole texts. Whole texts communicate a writer's ideas to an audience.

Writers can add meaning to texts using a variety of special language effects. Special language effects include voice (active voice or passive voice), figurative language, persuasive language and technical language.

A thorough understanding of what grammar is, and how it works, is vital for any writer, as it allows them to build texts successfully and to communicate clearly to a reader.

Language Features

Nouns

Nouns are words in a sentence that tell *who*, *where* or *what*. There are many different types of nouns that can be used in writing.

Common nouns

Common nouns are general names given to people, places and things.

The **doctor** at the **hospital** gave me some **medicine**.

Some **children** enjoy building **sandcastles** at the **beach**.

Abstract nouns

Abstract nouns are used to name ideas and feelings; things that people can imagine or think about, but cannot touch.

Kirra expressed her **opinion** on the **issue** discussed at the meeting.

The rescuers at the scene of the accident showed great **compassion** and **concern** for the injured tourists.

Concrete nouns

Some nouns are called concrete nouns because they represent physical objects that can be seen and touched rather than abstract qualities.

Grammar Note

Nouns can be 'countable' or 'uncountable'. Countable nouns represent individual people, animals, places, things or ideas that can be counted, e.g. two dogs, lots of photographs, several paintings.

Uncountable nouns are not individual objects, and therefore cannot be counted, e.g. juice, information, garbage.

Collective nouns

Collective nouns name groups of people, animals and things. Collective nouns are also a type of common noun.

The **audience** clapped loudly when the performance was finished.

A **swarm** of grasshoppers attacked the farmer's crop.

Dev bought a **bunch** of bananas at the supermarket.

It is important to remember that a collective noun is a single group made up of a number of members or objects. Therefore, when the collective noun is used in a sentence, it must have a singular verb. For example:

The team need one more goal to win the match. (incorrect)

The team needs one more goal to win the match. (correct)

The bunch of bananas weren't ripe yet. (incorrect)

The bunch of bananas wasn't ripe yet. (correct)

See page 66 for a list of collective nouns.

Compound nouns

There are three different types of compound nouns:

- closed or solid – comprises two words with no space between them, e.g. bathroom, keyhole, butterfly
- open or spaced – two separate words with a space between them, e.g. swimming pool, full moon, soccer boots
- hyphenated – two or more words separated by a hyphen, e.g. kick-off, daughter-in-law.

Proper nouns

Proper nouns are particular names given to people, places and things. Proper nouns always begin with a capital letter.

Kai and **Anika** quickly made a plan to save the tree.

Elephants can be found in **Africa** and **Asia**.

The guests arrived at the **Ocean Planet Hotel** and were greeted warmly by the **Hotel Manager**, **Adam**.

Within a short time, **Grace** and her crew from **Air Rescue** had their helicopter hovering over the scene.

Technical nouns

Technical nouns are nouns that are used in a particular area of study, or that relate to a specific topic, e.g. oxygen, eucalypt, astronomer. They are generally used in informative texts to provide accurate information.

Noun groups

Noun groups are groups of words that tell who, where or what is involved in the text. Descriptive details can be included to provide additional information about a noun, such as *how many*, *what is it like* and *what type is it*. A noun group may include articles, adjectives, pronouns and nouns.

The fluffy black kittens were asleep in a basket.

All the fans at **the music festival** sang and danced to **their favourite songs**.

Grammar Note

Nouns are often used with the words *the*, *a* and *an*. *The* is called a definite article because it describes a particular noun. *A* and *an* are called indefinite articles because they describe general nouns.

Most nouns in the English language do not have grammatical gender, although some nouns traditionally had different forms. These days, people usually prefer more neutral forms.

male form	female form	neutral form
chairman	chairwoman	chairperson
policeman	policewoman	police officer
actor	actress	actor
air steward	air stewardess	flight attendant
fireman	firewoman	firefighter

Pronouns

Pronouns replace nouns or noun groups. They are used to avoid repetition of a noun in a sentence or a paragraph.

Indefinite pronouns

Indefinite pronouns are used to refer to unspecified objects or people. They can be singular or plural.

A singular indefinite pronoun uses a singular verb, and a plural indefinite pronoun uses a plural verb.

These are some common indefinite pronouns:

somebody	anybody	nobody	everybody
someone	anyone	no one	everyone
something	anything	nothing	everything
somewhere	anywhere	nowhere	everywhere

Interrogative pronouns

Interrogative pronouns introduce questions that seek information. The interrogative pronouns are *what*, *which*, *who*, *whom* and *whose.*

Which book did you choose to read?

Who owns that shiny red scooter?

Note that some interrogative pronouns can be used as relative pronouns. If the pronoun is not part of a question, then it is not an interrogative pronoun.

Personal pronouns

Personal pronouns are used to replace the names of people and things. Some personal pronouns are *I*, *me*, *we*, *us*, *you*, *he*, *him*, *she*, *her*, *it*, *they* and *them.*

I didn't know Nur very well before **I** joined the athletics team. **She** lives on the other side of town. Now, **we** are best friends.

Alpacas have a long neck, large eyes and pointed ears. **They** have two large toes on each foot.

Grammar Note

Pronouns must agree in gender with the nouns they replace.

Dad went outside to do some gardening. I decided to help **him** by getting the seedlings to plant some herbs.

Jessica's car was **her** pride and joy. **She** washed **it** every weekend.

First-person pronouns

First-person pronouns are used when writers write or characters speak from a personal viewpoint. First-person pronouns include *I*, *me*, *my*, *we*, *us*, *our* and *ours*.

In **our** class today, **we** will learn how to make a birthday card for a friend.

I took **my** dog to the vet when it was unwell.

Second-person pronouns

Second-person pronouns are used when writers write dialogue for characters or when writers directly address the reader. Second-person pronouns include *you*, *your* and *yours*.

"**You** make me laugh," said Mason.

Put **your** hand inside the puppet. Move **your** fingers up and down.

"My name is Chandika," replied the girl. "What's **yours**?"

Third-person pronouns

Third-person pronouns are used to refer to people and things. They include *he*, *him*, *his*, *she*, *her*, *hers*, *it*, *its*, *they*, *them*, *their* and *theirs*.

He knew the other players were fantastic, so **he** wasn't surprised when **they** won the game.

The tall, straight tree trunk gets narrower as **it** rises.

Sometimes **they** put **their** own lives at risk to save others.

Grammar Note

Gender pronouns are the words people choose to refer to themselves that reflect their gender identity.

Knowing and using a person's correct pronouns makes them feel respected and valued.

- *He/him/his*: used for someone who identifies as male or masculine.
- *She/her/hers:* used for someone who identifies as female or feminine.
- *They/them/theirs*: used for someone who chooses not to or does not identify with male or female gender.

Possessive pronouns

Possessive pronouns are used to show ownership. Some possessive pronouns are *my, mine, our, ours, your, yours, her, hers, his, its, their* and *theirs*.

"Take off **your** muddy shoes!" said Mum.

After lunch, Dilip and **his** friend made a volcano for their science project.

As we approached, the rabbit scurried into **its** burrow.

Relative pronouns

Relative pronouns connect different parts of a sentence by replacing a word or phrase. They are placed next to the nouns they refer to. The relative pronouns are *that, which, who, whom* and *whose*.

On Saturday morning, Ali and Dad saw a huge tree **that** had fallen over in the park.

In the example below, the two sentences are combined into one sentence by replacing *The dirtiness of the water* with *which*.

When water levels fall too low, the water becomes dirty. The dirtiness of the water can lead to disease.

When water levels fall too low, the water becomes dirty, **which** can lead to disease.

Grammar Note

Some pronouns, which are called demonstrative pronouns, are determiners, e.g. *this, that, these, those*. Sometimes they are referred to as demonstrative adjectives. They can also be placed before a noun to tell the reader what the noun is referring to.

I read **that** book in one afternoon.

Those grapes are really delicious!

Adjectives

Adjectives describe nouns, pronouns and other adjectives. Different types of adjectives can be grouped according to the information they provide. Sometimes adjectives are written immediately before the noun they describe, and sometimes they are written after the noun.

Classifying adjectives

Classifying adjectives give information about the characteristics or qualities of nouns and pronouns.

They wore **colourful** costumes and danced enthusiastically.

I saw a **bright**, **flashing** light above us.

A ranger was checking the tree for any **injured** animals.

Comparative and superlative adjectives

Big, *bigger* and *biggest* are examples of adjectives that can compare the words they describe. In these examples, *big* is described as being the positive form (or degree), *bigger* is the comparative form and *biggest* is in the superlative form.

When the comparative form is used, the writer is making a comparison between two items.

My dog is **bigger** than your dog.

When the superlative form is used, the writer is making a comparison among three or more objects.

This is a photo of the **oldest** man in the world.

Generally, if an adjective has one syllable, the comparative and superlative forms are made by adding –*er* and –*est*.

Grammar Note

A syllable is a single unit of spoken language that contains one vowel sound. This sound can be made by a vowel or combination of vowels, or the letter –*y*, as in *happy*. A syllable can have one or more letters. Words can have one or more syllables.

- girl (one syllable)
- children (two syllables: *chil* + *dren*)
- family (three syllables: *fam* + *i* + *ly*)

word type	rule	positive	comparative	superlative
One syllable	Make comparative and superlative forms by adding *–er* and *–est*	old	old**er**	old**est**
		long	long**er**	long**est**
One syllable and ends in *–e*	Make comparative and superlative forms by adding *–r* and *–st*	nice	nice**r**	nice**st**
		large	large**r**	large**st**
Ends with a vowel followed by a consonant	The consonant is doubled before adding *–er* or *–est*	big	big**ger**	big**gest**
		hot	hot**ter**	hot**test**
Ends with a consonant followed by *–y*	the *–y* is changed to *–i* before adding *–er* or *–est*	happy	happ**ier**	happ**iest**
		silly	sill**ier**	sill**iest**
Two syllables, ending in *–le* or *–ow*	Use the *–er* or *–est* endings	gentle	gentle**r**	gentle**st**
		narrow	narrow**er**	narrow**est**
Most other two-syllable adjectives	Use the words *more* or *most*	peaceful	**more** peaceful	**most** peaceful
		pleasant	**more** pleasant	**most** pleasant
More than two syllables	Use the words *more* or *most*	delicious	**more** delicious	**most** delicious
		important	**more** important	**most** important
Exceptions	Some adjectives change to different words	good	better	best
		many	more	most

Demonstrative adjectives

The demonstrative adjectives are *this*, *that*, *these* and *those*. They are used to refer to the distance between the objects or people, and the speaker.

This and *these* refer to people or objects that are close by; *that* and *those* are used for people and objects that are further away.

This costume is the one you will wear in the school play and **that** costume is the one Charlie will wear.

The audience will sit on **these** chairs for the performance, while the teachers will sit on **those** benches at the back.

I will buy **that** dress to wear to the party because it matches **these** shoes.

Those bananas have gone soft; take **this** one to have with your lunch.

The adjectives *this* and *that* modify singular nouns; *these* and *those* modify plural nouns.

This ice-cream is delicious!

We will share **that** pizza between us.

These songs are my favourite ones.

The latest models are **those** phones over there.

Demonstrative adjectives always come first in adjective order. For example:

This big, hairy dog is very friendly.

Archie took **those** old faded blue denim jeans to the op shop.

Cara was given **that** small elegant silver bracelet and **those** black suede high-heeled lace-up boots for her birthday.

Factual adjectives

Factual adjectives describe facts about nouns, such as colour, size or shape.

Inside the temple is a statue of an **enormous golden** Buddha.

They are found in very **dry** places in **southern** Africa.

Meerkats have **furry** bodies, with **large** eyes and **long** legs.

Indefinite adjectives

Indefinite adjectives describe the noun in an unspecified way. They do not refer to any particular person, place or thing.

Many people enjoy dining at restaurants.

Other examples of indefinite adjectives are: *some*, *each*, *various*, *few*, *other*, *enough*.

Numbering adjectives

Numbering adjectives describe quantity. Cardinal numbers (one, four, ten) are usually classified as determiners and are generally not recognised as adjectives. But words indicating unspecified numbers are considered adjectives.

Many people visit the markets to buy fresh food and other goods.

Some video games have incredible special effects.

Ordinal numbers relating to position are also adjectives.

Yun was the **first** person to arrive at school this morning.

Opinion adjectives

Opinion adjectives describe how the writer feels about something.

We both had an **exciting** time.

Roll clouds are **amazing** and **beautiful** clouds.

I think this is a **clever** artwork because it makes people think in **different** ways.

Possessive adjectives

Possessive adjectives indicate ownership.

He flapped **his** powerful wings, and flew steadily upwards.

They help keep **their** mob safe and strong by living, hunting and playing together.

Lily caught the early bus to school with **her** big sister, Jelena.

Verbs

There are many different types of verbs. Verbs provide information about the action or state of the subject in a sentence.

Grammar Note

The subject of a sentence is the person or thing that the sentence is about.

Action verbs

Action verbs describe the subject's movements or behaviour.

Today, many people **work** from home.

I **packed** a bag with clothes.

Pour the milk slowly into the blender.

Compound verbs

Compound verbs are verbs made up of more than one word.

The tools people communicate with **have changed** over time.

It **will protect** your head if you have an accident.

We **should be allowed** to choose the clothes we wear to school.

Modal verbs

Modal verbs express what may, can or might happen. They are used in combination with other verbs.

First, if we spend less time playing video games or watching TV, we **can** have fun with our family.

She **might** visit us later.

But I think we **should** have bins in the school ground.

The most common modal verbs are *can*, *could*, *may*, *might*, *shall*, *will*, *must*, *should* and *would*.

Some modal verbs have a special form when used in the negative form: *cannot*, *can't*, *couldn't*, *mightn't*, *shan't*, *shouldn't*, *won't*, *wouldn't*.

Phrasal verbs

Phrasal verbs combine a verb with an adverb or preposition.

It would be great **to catch up** with you at the weekend.

Please **fill in** the form so I have a record of your name and address.

Our car **broke down** just two blocks from our house.

Relating verbs

Relating verbs link information about the subject and its action, behaviour or characteristics.

Paper wasps **are** insects.

Yesterday **was** a special day.

Sensing verbs

Sensing verbs express the subject's feelings.

I **think** it is very important to follow bike safety rules when you are riding your bike.

Lan **believes** that being a vegetarian helps the environment.

I sometimes **feel** melancholy on cold and rainy days.

Verbs and agreement

Agreement is a grammatical term for the correct link between the subject and verb in a sentence. Verbs must change their form to have agreement.

The subject and verb must agree in *person* (*first*, *second* or *third person*).

agreement in person	
person	**agreeing verb**
first-person **singular**	I **am** going to bake a cake.
first-person **plural**	We **are** going to bake a cake.
second-person **singular**	You **are** going to bake a cake.
second-person **plural**	You and Noah **are** going to bake a cake.
third-person **singular**	Noah **is** going to bake a cake.
third-person **plural**	They **are** going to bake a cake.

The subject and verb must also agree in number.

agreement in number	
A singular subject must have a singular verb.	I **play** basketball at school. He **plays** basketball at school.
A plural subject must have a plural verb.	Linh and Yarran **play** basketball at school.
Collective nouns must have a singular verb for agreement, as the collective noun is considered to be in singular form.	The team **plays** football at school.

Grammar Note

Singular means *one*. Nouns, pronouns and verbs can have singular forms.

Plural means *more than one*. Nouns, pronouns and verbs can have plural forms.

Verb tenses

Verbs also change form when they are written in different tenses. In grammar, tense refers to the time when an action or event happened. Generally, there are three main tenses: past, present and future.

past tense	
Verbs written in past tense tell about things that have already happened.	We **had** friends for dinner. (simple past tense) We **were having** eggs for breakfast. (continuous past tense) We **had eaten** all the strawberries. (perfect past tense)

>>

present tense	
Verbs written in present tense tell about things that are happening now.	We **have** ten children at our house for the day. (simple present tense) We **are having** eggs for breakfast. (continuous present tense) We **have eaten** all the strawberries. (perfect present tense)
future tense	
Verbs written in future tense tell about things that have not yet happened.	We **will have** friends over for dinner. (simple future tense) We **will be having** friends over for dinner. (continuous future tense)

Adverbs

Adverbs add meaning to verbs by telling *how*, *where*, *when* or *why*. Adverbs can also add meaning to adjectives and other adverbs.

Adverbs of manner tell ***how***:

They move **quickly** across the deepest parts of the ocean.

Sometimes, meerkats will work **together** to scare a predator away.

I stood in line and waited **patiently**.

Adverbs of place tell ***where***:

Rabbits live **underground** in burrows made up of lots of tunnels.

My whole family was **there**.

The tins rolled **everywhere**.

Adverbs of time tell ***when***:

Always try your best.

Now, we add the chopped tomatoes.

This happens **early** in the morning or **late** in the day

Adverbs of reason tell ***why***:

Elephants are endangered, **therefore** it is illegal to hunt them.

Rani was a great role model; **consequently**, she was elected to the position of school captain.

Adverb intensifiers

Intensifiers are used to increase the impact of adjectives, other adverbs or sentences. Examples include *extremely*, *most*, *much*, *really* and *very*.

Being a helicopter pilot can be a satisfying but **extremely** dangerous job.

Vijayrathna can run **very** quickly.

The children **thoroughly** enjoyed their school excursion.

I didn't want to go to athletics training when I had a test the next day. **Surely** the coach would understand.

Adverb modifiers

Modifiers are used to lessen the impact of adjectives, other adverbs or sentences. Examples include *almost*, *just* and *only*.

We were **almost** asleep when the alarm sounded.

Ava invited **only** twenty people to the party.

Comparative and superlative adverbs

Adverbs have three forms that are used for making comparisons: *positive*, *comparative* and *superlative*.

Adverbs that do not end in –*ly* make their comparative and superlative forms by adding –*er* and –*est*. If the adverb ends in –*e*, then –*r* and –*st* are added. For the adverb *early*, change the –*y* to –*i* and then add –*er* or –*est*.

Comparative and superlative adverbs are often made by adding the word endings –*er* and –*est*. Sometimes the word *more* or *most* is put before adverbs to compare them.

Some adverbs change to different words to show degree, e.g. *badly*, *worse*, *worst*.

word type	rule	positive	comparative	superlative
Does not end in *–ly*	Make comparative and superlative forms by adding *–er* and *–est*, or *-r* and *-st* if adverb ends in *-e*	soon	soon**er**	soon**est**
		fast	fast**er**	fast**est**
		low	low**er**	low**est**
		late	late**r**	late**st**
Ends in *–ly*	Use the words *more* or *most*	happily	**more** happily	**most** happily
		swiftly	**more** swiftly	**most** swiftly
		greedily	**more** greedily	**most** greedily
		efficiently	**more** efficiently	**most** efficiently
Exception ending in *–ly*	Change *y* to *i* and add *–er* and *–est*	early	earl**ier**	earl**iest**
Other exceptions	Change to different words	badly	worse	worst
		much	more	most
		less	lesser	least

Conjunctions

Conjunctions join other words, phrases or clauses in a sentence. When they are used to join clauses, conjunctions can also be placed at the beginning of a sentence. Conjunctions include *and, because, but, for, or, since, so, though*.

Trees, buildings, people **and** animals can make shadows.

Bacon **and** eggs with smashed avocado is a popular breakfast.
('and' joins words)

I usually do my homework in the office **or** at the table.

('or' joins phrases)

Nonna helped Luca look outside for the little possum, **but** they couldn't find it.

Tala has been invited to a party on Saturday afternoon, **but** she will be playing in her football final instead.

('but' joins clauses)

My whole family was there, **so** one table was not big enough.
('so' joins clauses)

Connectives

Connectives join ideas in clauses, sentences or paragraphs within a text. They include *also*, *for example*, *however*, *in fact*, *soon*, *then*.

Frank can be shy sometimes, **however**, he is very friendly.

In conclusion, children and adults should visit the dentist on a regular basis.

Prepositions

Prepositions are usually placed before a noun, pronoun or phrase. Many prepositions show the time, place or position of something. They also connect different parts of sentences. Prepositions include *about, along, among, at, behind, between, down, during, from, in, inside, near, on, out, to, through, up, with*.

Where Is Coco? is a funny movie **about** a talking dog who gets lost **at** the shops.

Put the strawberries **into** the blender **with** the banana.

Long ago, children used fountain pens and ink to write **in** their books.

Phrases

Phrases are groups of words that form parts of sentences. They have meaning in a sentence, but cannot stand alone as they don't make sense by themselves.

At my next attempt, I succeeded in righting the sail **of my windsurfer**, and then, **to my amazement**, a bird landed **on the board behind me**!

Adjectival phrases

Adjectival phrases add information to nouns. They often begin with a preposition.

The new owners **of the farm** were diligent workers.

Both breeds **with a good sense of smell** were used as tracker dogs.

Adverbial phrases

Adverbial phrases add information to verbs. They often begin with a preposition.

Venomous snakes are found **all over the world**.

"The weather's deteriorating quickly," Rebecca said **in a worried tone**.

During rescue missions, the pilot constantly checks weather and flight conditions.

Prepositional phrases

A prepositional phrase is a phrase that begins with a preposition. Some adverbial and adjectival phrases are also prepositional phrases.

We set up the picnic **on the grass**.

Many species of butterflies were found **in the forest**.

Time and sequence words and phrases

Time and sequence words and phrases are used to connect events in order (*first*, *next*, *finally*) or to indicate time (*in the morning*) or that a period of time has passed (*last year*).

Next, I beat the eggs.

"We're going on a road trip," Mum said to me **last night**.

During the next three months, the nymph sheds its skin four times.

Building Texts

Sentences

Sentences are groups of words that express an idea. They have a subject and a verb. Sentences begin with a capital letter and end with a full stop, an exclamation mark or a question mark.

Simple sentences

Simple sentences contain one complete idea that makes sense by itself.

The little frogs swam in the pond.

Gabe received a new video game for his birthday.

Compound sentences

Compound sentences have two parts. Each part contains an idea that makes sense by itself. The parts are joined by a conjunction.

An adult female lays new eggs and the life cycle starts again.

idea | **conjunction** | **idea**

Dan left the front door open so he could carry in the shopping bags.

idea | **conjunction** | **idea**

Grammar Note

Some writers deliberately use sentences that don't have verbs. These are called sentence fragments and are used in direct speech or for dramatic effect.

"Can I come around to your place?"

"Not now."

The kitten they found in the drain was mewing pitifully. **Obviously terrified.**

Complex sentences

Complex sentences have two or more parts. One part contains the main idea, and makes sense by itself. The other parts contain more information that builds on the main idea. This extra information does not make sense by itself.

We had lunch at my cousin's house to celebrate Eid ul-Fitr,

main idea

although I think my parents are better cooks.

extra information

When the sun shines on a tree, the tree blocks the light.

extra information | **main idea**

Grammar Note

The main idea is called an *independent clause* or a main clause. The extra information is called a *dependent clause* or subordinate clause.

Clauses

Clauses are groups of words that have a subject and a verb. Clauses can form a whole sentence or part of a sentence.

Main (or independent) clauses

Main (or independent) clauses make sense by themselves. They may be complete sentences or part of a sentence.

I wore a new shirt.

Two independent clauses can be joined with a conjunction to make one longer sentence.

She has big, white teeth, too, but she won't bite!

Subordinate (or dependent) clauses

Subordinate (or dependent) clauses do not make sense by themselves, but rely on main (or independent) clauses to complete sentences. A subordinate clause adds extra information to the main clause.

A helmet will protect your head, if you have an accident.

independent **dependent**

Adverbial clauses

Adverbial clauses add meaning to the verb in the main (or independent) clause. They tell *how*, *when*, *where* or *why*. They are a form of subordinate clause.

If we all pack a waste-free lunch, we can help keep our school clean.

My parents will make sure I go to bed on time, **so I am well rested for school**.

Adjectival clauses

Adjectival clauses add meaning to nouns or pronouns in main (or independent) clauses. They are a form of subordinate clause.

Cats **that get plenty of exercise** stay fit and healthy.

Although Waru was the newest member of the team, he was so skilful he was chosen to be captain.

Types of sentences

There are many different types of sentences that can be used in different texts. For more information about text types, see Chapter 5.

Statements

Statements provide particular information about a subject. They end with a full stop. Statements are the most common type of sentence and are used in most text types.

Jupiter is the biggest planet in our solar system.

Pour the smoothie into two glasses.

Topic sentences

Topic sentences are usually the first and most important sentence in a paragraph because they contain the main idea. The other sentences in the paragraph provide additional information and expand on the main idea presented in the topic sentence.

Roll clouds may form in some places when there are storms and the wind blows in strong gusts. They may form in other places when sea breezes blow. Sometimes, several roll clouds move across the sky, one after the other.

Cause-and-effect sentences

Cause-and-effect sentences indicate that when one event occurs (the 'cause'), it causes another event (the 'effect') to follow. Cause-and-effect sentences are useful in explanations.

When we are cold, we automatically shiver to try to warm ourselves up.

cause (When we are cold) — **effect** (we automatically shiver to try to warm ourselves up)

When an undersea earthquake happens,

cause

large waves form on the ocean above its centre.

effect

Questions

Questions end with a question mark. Questions are often found in Narratives, Expositions and Discussions.

"What did you do over the weekend**?**" asked Chona.

Do birds always nest in trees**?**

Grammar Note

Rhetorical questions are questions that either don't require an answer, or are answered by the speaker or writer. Rhetorical questions are used to encourage readers to think about different aspects of the topic, and are commonly found in Expositions and Discussions.

Who doesn't love pizza?

Commands

Commands give an order or direction. They end with a full stop or an exclamation mark. Commands often begin with a verb. They are used in Procedures and Narratives.

Go to a lake or beach with calm water.

"**Watch** where you're going!" shouted Aisha.

Exclamations

Exclamations are used in Narratives to express a strong feeling or emotion, and in Expositions to express a particular point of view. They end with an exclamation mark.

"I love this song**!**" exclaimed Omar.

Then, at last, the International Space Station appeared**!**

"Move back**!**" warned Benji. "You are too close to the edge."

Speech

Speech refers to words that have been spoken. There are two main types of speech: direct speech and reported speech.

Direct speech

Direct speech, also called dialogue, refers to the words spoken by a person or character in a text. In writing, direct speech is placed inside quotation marks. Direct speech can be at the beginning, middle or end of a sentence, or can be separated by other words that name the speaker or explain how the words have been spoken. The first word in direct speech always begins with a capital letter. Direct speech is often used by characters in Narratives, and in Expositions to quote an argument in support of a topic.

The lifeguard said, "Make sure you swim between the two flags!"

"A new virtual reality game!" said Leo. "That's interesting."

"Follow the yellow brick road!" was the instruction given to Dorothy.

Reported speech

Reported speech is used to write what a person or character says, without using direct speech. Reported speech does not use quotation marks. Reported speech is mostly used in Recounts, Narratives, Expositions and Discussions.

Our teacher told us to line up to go to the library.

I mentioned that we were going to the beach at the weekend.

The salesman recommended that we buy a spare battery for the new drill.

Paragraphs

Paragraphs are groups of sentences about a common theme. Usually, the topic sentence is the first sentence in a paragraph. The sentences that follow provide additional, supporting information about the same subject.

New paragraphs are used for each new idea or thought. Text connectives can help the text flow from one paragraph to another.

The orca is a large sea animal. Orcas live in oceans around the world. The orca is sometimes called a killer whale.

An orca has a black and white body. It has two flippers and a wide tail. The fin on its back is tall and straight. It has a blowhole on its head for breathing air.

An orca has strong jaws and long, sharp teeth. It eats fish, seals and sea lions. Some orcas eat penguins and other seabirds, too.

Special Language Effects

Writers can use language in many different ways to create special effects. These effects help to build meaning in texts.

Voice

Voice is a grammatical term used to refer to the types of verbs used in a piece of writing. Voice can be either active or passive. Active voice is more commonly used because it makes the writing more dynamic, and the characters seem more powerful.

Active voice

In active voice, the subject of the sentence performs the action.

In some sports, players score goals.

subject (players) **active verb** (score)

When active verbs are used, the subject of the sentence seems powerful because the subject is doing the action.

Passive voice

In passive voice, the action is being done to the subject.

The flat tyre was changed by Mia.

subject (flat tyre) **passive verb** (was changed)

When passive verbs are used, the subject of the sentence sounds weaker, as the action is being done *to* the subject.

> *Grammar Note*
>
> *Voice* is sometimes used to describe the author's idea or opinion expressed in a text.

Figurative language

Figurative language describes a range of special language effects that can be used to create vivid imagery in a piece of writing. These effects are more commonly used in Narratives, Recounts and poetry. They include alliteration, idioms, metaphors, onomatopoeia, personification and similes.

Alliteration

Alliteration is the repeated use of one or more letters at the beginning of words in the same phrase or sentence.

The **T**une of the **T**ulips

Lowanna's **l**azy **l**izard **l**ay on the **l**awn.

The **s**isters **s**lept **s**oundly.

Rabbits **r**oamed **r**ecklessly at **r**andom.

Freddie's **F**urry **F**riends **F**armhouse

Idioms

Idioms are phrases in which the whole phrase takes on a different meaning to the words themselves.

When I was called to the principal's office, I felt as though **my back was against the wall**.

I was **on cloud nine** when I received the results of my latest assessment task.

idiom	*meaning*
a piece of cake	very easy
beat around the bush	to avoid talking about what's really important
burn your bridges	to do something that makes it impossible to go back to the start
by the skin of your teeth	only just making it or getting by
cut corners	to do something in an easier or less expensive way

>>

idiom	*meaning*
every cloud has a silver lining	bad things one day eventually lead to good things
go back to the drawing board	to start something back at the very beginning
heart of gold	a way of describing someone who is very kind and generous
hit the books	to study very intensively
hit the nail on the head	to get something exactly right
keep an ear to the ground	to stay informed and updated about an issue
look before you leap	to consider the risks before moving ahead
more than you can poke a stick at	a large quantity of something
on thin ice	in a dangerous or risky situation
run around in circles	to put effort into something that does not create a worthwhile result
sell like hotcakes	to sell very quickly
step up your game	to start performing better
get out of hand	to become out of control
miss the boat	to come too late for something; to let an opportunity go due to inattention or lack of time
pull someone's leg	to make something up as a way of joking with someone

Grammar Note

Clichés are common expressions that have been overused and that most people know. When used in writing, they can sometimes weaken the meaning of a text by making the writing predictable. It is better to keep writing fresh and original by avoiding clichés, unless they form part of a character's dialogue.

"I felt like **a fish out of water**," said Ethan, after he'd played his first game of football.

"I'll be ready to leave at the **drop of a hat**," said Shakira.

"I **put two and two together** to solve the crime," said the detective.

Metaphors

Metaphors are used in writing or speaking to help explain something by comparing it to something else that is familiar to the audience. A metaphor (word or phrase) is applied to an object or action to which it would not usually be associated. It directly refers to one thing by mentioning another. Metaphors do not contain the words *as* or *like*.

Metaphors help people visualise unfamiliar ideas, and explain unfamiliar situations in a more meaningful way. They are used to add variety and interest to a person's writing or conversations by creating strong mental images.

Examples of metaphors are:

I recall the day I first went to boarding school; I experienced **a roller-coaster of emotions**.	Ben's temper was **a volcano** ready to explode.
He is **a night owl**.	Miksha's lovely voice was **music to his ears**.
She is **a shining star** on that stage.	The world is **a stage**.
The moon was **a white balloon** floating over the city.	At recess, the playground becomes **a circus**.

>>

The road ahead was **a ribbon** stretching across the desert.	Books are **the keys** to your imagination.
The park was **a lake** after the rain.	Your brain is **a computer**.
The sun is **a golden ball**.	She is **a walking dictionary**.
The lightning flashes were **fireworks in the sky**.	He got lost in **a sea of memories**.
The stars are **sparkling diamonds**.	The car was **an oven** from being parked in the sun.

Onomatopoeia

Onomatopoeia is a word or the use of a word that imitates the sound made by the person, animal or object in the text.

Bang! Crash!

beep, boom, buzz, clang, crack, hiss, honk, meow, scratch, sniff, splash, thump, vroom, whack, whoosh, zap

Personification

Personification is a language effect that gives human qualities to animals, objects and ideas. This can be done by using human names, feelings or actions.

Examples of personification are:

The **thunder grumbled**, warning of the storm to come.	The **bees played hide-and-seek** with the flowers as they buzzed from one to another.
The **sun glared at me** from high up in the sky.	The **river swallowed** the earth as the water continued to rise higher and higher.
The **sun smiled down** on us.	The **flowers waltzed** in the gentle breeze.

>>

The **light danced** on the surface of the water.	Mei's **life wandered** past.
The run-down **house appeared depressed**.	The **words leapt off** the paper as Anna read the story.
The first **rays of morning light tiptoed** through the field.	The **chocolate bar begged** me to eat it.

Similes

Similes are phrases that compare one thing with another, often beginning with *as* or *like*.

The land in the outback was **as flat as a pancake**.

This costume is ideal because it **fits like a glove**!

Some examples of common similes:

as boring as watching paint dry	as quiet as a mouse
as bright as a button	as slippery as an eel
as busy as a bee	as slow as a tortoise
as clear as crystal	as smooth as velvet
as cool as a cucumber	as steady as a rock
as cunning as a fox	as straight as an arrow
as dry as a bone	as strong as an ox
as fit as a fiddle	as tall as a skyscraper
as fresh as a daisy	as thin as a rake
as gentle as a lamb	as white as a ghost
as heavy as lead	as wise as an owl
as light as a feather	climbs like a monkey

>>

as proud as a peacock	slept like a baby
as quick as lightning	swims like a fish

Evaluative language

Evaluative language refers to the words used by an author to show judgement or to express an opinion. Evaluative language is often used in Recounts, Descriptions and Information Reports. Evaluative words can be adjectives, verbs or adverbs, and can express positive or negative feelings.

Pandas are **amazing** animals that **thoroughly deserve** our protection.

I found the concert **extremely boring**, as none of my **favourite** bands were playing.

Persuasive language

Persuasive language is used in writing to convince readers to accept or agree with a particular point of view. This is done by using words that convey personal feelings or opinions, such as abstract nouns, opinion adjectives, sensing verbs, and adverbs of manner and reason. Persuasive language is often used in Expositions, Discussions and Responses.

The floral arrangement at the entrance to the building was **exquisite**.

Some people **genuinely don't care** about the state of the environment.

Technical language

Technical language refers to the special words and phrases related to a topic. These words and phrases help the writer to provide accurate information in texts. Relating verbs, classifying and factual adjectives and noun groups are useful language features to include in technical writing. Technical language is most suitable for Descriptions, Explanations and Information Reports.

Tsunamis form when an undersea volcano **erupts**, or when there is an undersea **landslide**.

The **burrows** help protect the meerkats from **predators** and hot weather.

2 Punctuation

There are many reasons for using punctuation in writing. It helps to make meaning clearer by breaking sentences into logical parts. Punctuation shows where to pause or stop at appropriate places, making texts easier to read and understand. Punctuation can also be used to show expression, or to show when characters are speaking.

Punctuation Marks

The following are the most common punctuation marks.

Apostrophes (')

Apostrophes indicate where a letter or letters have been left out of a contraction. For more information on contractions, see page 51.

"**It's** time for our dinner now," said Joseph.

"**I'm** going to Germany, and **I'll** be gone for a month."

Apostrophes can also be used to show possession, or ownership; they show that something belongs to someone or something. The apostrophe is placed immediately after the owner in both singular and plural forms.

Auntie sat in the **driver's** seat. (The seat belongs to the driver.)

At the end of winter, the **wood frog's** heart starts to beat again. (The heart belongs to the wood frog.)

Baby gorillas sleep with their mother and they drink their **mother's** milk. (The milk belongs to their mother.)

Young baboons are too little to jump or swing by themselves, so they ride on their **mothers'** backs. (The backs belong to the mothers.)

Brackets

There are different types of brackets. They have different purposes in different types of texts.

Angle brackets < >

Angle brackets are used to indicate a website URL in written text.

Find more information at <cengage.com.au/primary>.

Curly brackets (or braces) { }

Curly brackets are often used in mathematics and technical writing. They can also be used to indicate that more than one word is being referred to at the same time.

The set of factors of 12 is {1, 2, 3, 4, 6, 12}

dairy products { milk
cheese

Round brackets (or parentheses) ( )

Round brackets are used when extra information is included in a sentence. The sentence must be grammatically correct even when the bracketed section is not read.

Manu decided to order a chocolate thickshake (although he usually had a caramel-flavoured one).

Round brackets are also used to indicate the source of quotations. A quotation is a group of words that was originally written or spoken by a person and is reused by another person.

I believe all parents and students should come along and enjoy our Friendship Art Display. (Effie Caridas – Year 6)

Round brackets can be used to refer to other parts of a written presentation.

Over the years, the number of koalas in the district has shown a noticeable decrease (see Table 1).

Round brackets can be used to introduce a shortened form of a group, state or organisation after it has been written in full.

Sydney is the capital of New South Wales (NSW).

The shortened form can then be used in the remainder of the text.

Round brackets can be used to enclose definitions or prompts for how to pronounce more difficult words.

cashmere (a type of wool)

pneumatic (say: *new-mat-ick*)

Round brackets can be used singularly or in pairs with numbers or letters to identify different items in a list.

You will need:

a) self-raising flour

b) milk

c) 2 eggs.

You will need:

(1) washing machine

(2) detergent

(3) clothes pegs.

Square brackets [ ]

Square brackets are used to include information that is not written by the author of the sentence. For example, a journalist may include the information to make the meaning clearer for readers. Square brackets are most commonly used in non-fiction texts, such as newspaper articles and essays.

The owner of the property [Whitegate Pty Ltd] submitted new plans to the council.

Bullet points (•)

Bullet points (also called dot points) are used to list items in a text. They can help with readability.

To make a salad sandwich, you will need:

- 2 slices of bread
- butter
- lettuce
- tomato
- grated cheese
- sliced cucumber
- grated carrot
- mayonnaise
- a plate
- a butter knife.

Capital letters (A, B, C)

A sentence always begins with a capital letter. Capital letters are also called upper-case letters.

Many monkeys and apes are in danger of extinction.

A capital letter is always used for a proper noun.

Chloe and her mum were staying with **G**ran and **P**oppa in **T**asmania.

A capital letter is also used for:

- the first-person pronoun **I**
- the first word in a line of poetry even if it is not a new sentence. (This is optional.)

Colons (:)

Colons are used to indicate that more details will follow what has already been written in a sentence.

The sign on the door read**:** Surgery.

Colons are also used to introduce items in a list.

You will need**:**

- a bucket of warm water
- dog shampoo
- an old towel
- a dog.

Commas (,)

Commas are used to separate words in a list. There is no comma before the word *and* before the last item in a list. Commas can also be used to separate phrases or clauses in a sentence. The use of a comma can help to clarify the meaning of the sentence.

The plans for the redeveloped area show city buildings**,** stadiums**,** parks and playgrounds.

Once the victim is still and calm**,** apply first-aid treatment.

Every Monday morning**,** Mr Lotti gave his class a special challenge.

Many of the trees are hundreds of years old**,** but some live to be more than 2000 years old.

In direct speech, when the speaker is named before the start of the dialogue, a comma is used to separate the two parts of the sentence.

Manoj said, "Do you know what we have forgotten to make?"

A comma can also be used where additional information is inserted in a sentence.

In winter, the coldest time of year, some animals cannot find enough food to eat.

Dashes (–)

Dashes are used to show a break or pause in a sentence.

The representative team was selected from over fifty players – and only the best were chosen!

Which flavour of ice cream do you prefer – chocolate or strawberry?

Dashes are also used to show that speech has been interrupted.

"I can't remember where –"
"Did you look under your bed?" queried Tala.

Ellipses (...)

Ellipses show that part or parts of a quotation have been omitted.

"When children count aloud by tens, they say ten, twenty, thirty, ... ninety, one hundred."

They can also be used to show a pause or that a line of text is incomplete.

"Why did you ... ?" asked the police officer.

Exclamation marks (!)

Exclamation marks are used to show strong feeling or emotion in a sentence.

Yolanda was a great yoga teacher!

Wow, that was an amazing movie!

They are also used in commands to show which words should be emphasised.

"Sit!" he ordered, tugging downwards on the dog's lead.

Full stops (.)

Full stops are used to show the end of a sentence. They are used for statements and some commands.

The train came to a stop at the station.

There were lots of people dancing at the festival.

Please give a warm welcome to our guest.

Hyphens (-)

Hyphens are used to indicate a break in a word, or a link between two or more words. Hyphens are used in:

- some compound adjectives, where the words together modify the noun

  The dish was prepared by a world-class chef.

- numbers, when used adjectivally

  The babies were two-and-a-half weeks old.

- pronunciation guides

  crias (say: *cree-yas*)

- word breaks (when the whole word will not fit on one line)

  They make their own beautiful clothing from the yarn.

When using a hyphen to break a word over two lines, always place the hyphen at the end of a syllable.

Question marks (?)

Question marks are placed at the end of sentences. They are used to show that a question is being asked. Words such as *What? When? Why? Who? Where? Which? How? Is? Are? Should? Could? Would? Can? May?* are common words used to begin questions.

"Which way is it to the zoo?" asked Dad.

"Are we going to visit Uncle?" Jiemba asked.

Would Sophia make it home?

Quotation marks (‘ ’) and (“ ”)

Quotation marks (or speech marks) are used to show words that are spoken or quoted. Either single or double quotation marks can be used, but whichever type is chosen must be used consistently within a text. Punctuation is placed before the closing quotation marks. Quotation marks are not used in reported speech.

‘It was so much fun!’ Ruby said.

“Thank you for taking care of me,” Fatima said. (direct speech)

Fatima thanked Ayla for taking care of her. (reported speech)

Quotation marks can also be placed around technical words or slang.

When we experience anxiety, three parts of our brain react in different ways: the “survival” part, the “emotional” part and the “smart” part.

Sometimes, song titles, article titles and chapter titles are written using quotation marks.

Semicolons (;)

Semicolons mark a break in the sentence; they are a stronger pause than a comma. Note that semicolons link ideas, but commas separate ideas.

The surgeon quickly prepared for a long session in theatre; this patient had multiple, serious injuries.

Semicolons are sometimes used to separate items in lists when the items have commas in them.

Amelia decided to sell some of her old stuff online: her old phone, laptop and game console; her backpack, last year’s schoolbooks and her guitar, which she hadn’t picked up all year; several T-shirts and some jeans that were too small for her; and a pair of sneakers she didn’t wear any more.

Slashes (/)

Slashes are mostly used to show alternatives (replacing the word *or*).

It was a simple question, needing just a yes/no answer.

The cafe offered scrambled eggs with bacon and/or sausages.

Slashes can also indicate the parts of something. They are used to surround letters that represent a particular sound.

the /f/ sound in *photograph*

Slashes are used in URLs to show pages and subpages.

cengage.com.au/primary

Slashes can be used in the shortened form of writing the date.

14/04/2025

Symbols

Symbols can be used to replace words in some types of written communication. These are some common symbols and their meaning.

symbol	name	meaning
&	ampersand	and
*	asterisk	star, or multiply
@	at sign	at, or to indicate domain names in email addresses, or to tag/ mention people on social media
#	number sign, hash	number, or for a hashtag on social media
%	per cent	per hundred parts
ea	each	each

3 Spelling

Spelling Knowledge

In order to be a good writer, it helps to know a range of spelling strategies that can be used when attempting to spell more difficult and less familiar words. It is not possible to be a competent speller by always relying on a single method of spelling unknown words.

Many everyday words we speak and write have been borrowed from other languages. These languages sometimes have a different set of rules for spelling. Thus, writing words in English has become a complicated blend of many different rules. As a result, there are many variations and inconsistencies in the way English words are written.

Knowledge of the following spelling skills will allow writers to draw on a range of strategies.

Visual knowledge: The way words and letter combinations look

Some words need to be learned by simply remembering the order of the letters they contain. Many of these words do not follow a spelling pattern, which can make them difficult to sound out and spell correctly.

have, they, their, height, through, knock

Phonological knowledge: The way words and letter combinations sound

Phonological knowledge refers to oral language and the understanding of the different ways language can be broken down into smaller parts. This knowledge about sounds in language is an important foundation for learning to spell. Students need to develop the ability to hear, identify and manipulate the smallest individual units of sound (phonemes) in spoken words, and match these with the appropriate written letters or letter combinations for each sound (graphemes). Activities using syllables, onset and rime, alliteration and rhyme can help to support students' knowledge in this area.

Phonemes and graphemes

Listening to the sounds in words is an important skill to learn for spelling words correctly. Many words can be spelt by sounding them out and knowing which letters, or combinations of letters, make those sounds.

Readers and writers rely on their knowledge of phonemes to hear the sounds contained in a word, and graphemes to write the sounds in the word.

c – a – t

b – o – x

d – i – g

Onset and rime

Learning about onset and rime is a way of writing words based on logical letter patterns. The 'onset' is the consonant or consonants that come before the vowel in a syllable, e.g. *b* is the onset in *ball*; *br* is the onset in *bright*. The 'rime' is the part of the syllable from the vowel onwards, e.g. *all* in *ball*, and *ight* in *bright*.

Consonant blends

Consonant blends are letter combinations where each consonant has an individual sound, e.g. *cl*, *dr*, *st*.

cl – a – p

dr – o – p

st – e – p

Consonant digraphs

Two consonants that work together to create one sound are called *consonant digraphs*, e.g. *sh*, *th*, *ng*. Learning and remembering the letters that create these sounds can be used to support attempts at spelling words correctly.

sh – i – p

th – i – n

r – i – ng

Vowel digraphs

Two vowels can also work together to create a single sound, called a *vowel digraph*, e.g. *ai*, *ea*, *ou*. Learning and remembering the vowel digraphs is another useful strategy in learning to spell less familiar words.

tr – ai – n

r – ea – ch

cl – ou – d

Spelling Note

When attempting to write a word correctly, it is important to know that different letter combinations can make the same sound.

g**ir**l, h**er**, t**ur**n, w**or**d

Morphemic knowledge: The way words change when they take on a different form

Often, longer words can be broken down into smaller parts. For example, *unhealthy* can be broken down into *un*– (a prefix), *health* (a base), and –*y* (a suffix). These smaller parts are called *morphemes*. Understanding how words can be broken into morphemes can help with the spelling of words that have the same base. Many new words can be made by adding prefixes or suffixes to the base.

excite – excited, excitedly, excitement, excites, exciting, unexcited

like – dislike, likeable, liked, likely, likes, liking, unlikely

Spelling Note

A prefix is a morpheme added to the beginning of a word to change its meaning.

possible – **im**possible

reliable – **un**reliable

>>

A suffix is a morpheme added to the end of a word to change its form.

real – real**ly**

beauty – beauti**ful**

A base has no prefixes or suffixes added to it.

For more information on adding prefixes and suffixes, see pages 46–8.

Etymological knowledge: The origin and history of words

Many words in the English language have been borrowed from the Greek and Latin languages. Understanding the meaning of some of these words can help with spelling. For example, *aqua* comes from the Latin for *water*, and is the common base for all these words:

aquamarine, **aqua**plane, **aqua**rium, **aqua**tic

Other useful bases that can be used to write more complex words, and their origins, are listed below and on the following page.

base	origin	meaning	words
anti	Greek	against	antibacterial, antidote
aster	Greek	star	asteroid, astronaut, astronomy
auto	Greek	self	autobiography, automatic
bio	Greek	life	biography, biology
geo	Greek	earth	geography, geology, geometry
graph	Greek	write	autograph, grapheme, graphic
hydro	Greek	water	dehydrate, hydrant, hydropower
path	Greek	feel	apathy, empathy
photo	Greek	light	photocopy, photograph, photon
tele	Greek	far	telepathy, telescope, television

>>

base	origin	meaning	words
aqua	Latin	water	aquatic, aquarium
audio	Latin	hear	audible, audience, auditorium
circum	Latin	round	circle, circulate, circumnavigate, circus
cooperio	Latin	cover over	coverage, discover, uncover
manus	Latin	hand	manicure, manipulate, manual, manuscript
pax	Latin	peace	pacific, pacifist, pacify
scribo	Latin	write	describe, proscribe, script
vacuus	Latin	empty	evacuate, vacate, vacuum
video	Latin	see	television, video, visible

Spelling Generalisations

Spelling generalisations are basic rules that help writers to spell less familiar words. Although there are many exceptions to these generalisations, they are useful to know. Following are some of the most common spelling generalisations.

Sounds

Sometimes the sound of a word can be a clue to how it may be spelt.

i before *e*, except after *c*

When the letters *e* and *i* are used to make an /ee/ sound, remember to use *i* before *e*, except after *c*:

ach**ie**ve, bel**ie**ve, br**ie**f, f**ie**ld, hyg**ie**ne, n**ie**ce, p**ie**ce, s**ie**ge, th**ie**f, t**ie**r

c**ei**ling, conc**ei**t, conc**ei**ve, dec**ei**t, rec**ei**pt

When the main vowel sounds like /ay/, use *ei*.

fr**ei**ght, n**ei**ghbour, r**ei**ns, sl**ei**gh, w**ei**gh, w**ei**ght, v**ei**n

Exceptions to the *i* before e generalisation include:

caff**ei**ne, consc**ie**nce, **ei**ther, for**ei**gn, l**ei**sure, prot**ei**n, spec**ie**s, suffic**ie**nt

ck at the end of a word

The letter combination *ck* only occurs after a short vowel sound:

ba**ck**, pa**ck**, qua**ck**, tra**ck**; de**ck**, ne**ck**, pe**ck**, wre**ck**; ki**ck**, li**ck**, qui**ck**, sti**ck**, tri**ck**; kno**ck**, lo**ck**, po**ck**et, so**ck**; du**ck**, lu**ck**, su**ck**, tru**ck**

k or *c* at the beginning of a word

For a /k/ sound at the beginning of a word, use a *k* if the vowel following is *e* or *i*, otherwise use *c*.

kennel, **k**ept, **k**ite, **k**itten; **c**age, **c**atch, **c**otton, **c**up

> *Spelling Note*
>
> Vowels are the following five letters of the alphabet: **a**, **e**, **i**, **o**, **u**
>
> Consonants are all the letters of the alphabet that are not vowels:
>
> **b**, **c**, **d**, **f**, **g**, **h**, **j**, **k**, **l**, **m**, **n**, **p**, **q**, **r**, **s**, **t**, **v**, **w**, **x**, **y**, **z**

Making plurals

Most words form the plural by adding –*s*.

paper + **s** = paper**s**

street + **s** = street**s**

To make a word plural when it ends in –*s*, –*ss*, –*sh*, –*ch*, or –*z*, add –*es*.

dress + **es** = dress**es**

wish + **es** = wish**es**

To make a word plural when it ends in –*y*, change the *y* to *i* and add –*es*.

baby – **y** + **i** + **es** = bab**ies**

To make a word plural that ends in –*f*, or –*fe*, change the *f* to *v* and then add –*es* or –*s*.

half – **f** + **v** + **es** = hal**ves**

knife – **f** + **v** + **s** = kni**ves**

(Exceptions: chief, chiefs; roof, roofs.)

Spelling Note

There are some exceptions to these rules: the plural of *goose* is *geese*, and the plural of *woman* is *women*.
Some nouns are the same in singular and plural form, such as *sheep*: one *sheep*; two *sheep*. Other nouns are always written in plural form, such as *scissors* and *trousers*.

Adding prefixes or suffixes

Adding *–able*

To add *–able* as a suffix, add it to a base.

remark + **able** = remark**able**

To add *–able* to a word that ends in *–e*, take off the *e* then add the suffix.

note – **e** + **able** = not**able**

desire – **e** + **able** = desir**able**

Adding *all–*

To add *all–* as a prefix to a base, take off one *l*.

all – **l** + most = **al**most

all – **l** + ways = **al**ways

Adding *–ed*

To add *–ed* as a suffix, add it to a base.

stay + **ed** = stay**ed**

employ + **ed** = employ**ed**

To add *–ed* to a word that has only one syllable and one short vowel sound, double the final consonant then add the suffix.

clap + **p** + **ed** = clap**ped**

To add *–ed* to a word that already ends in *e*, do not add *–ed*; add *–d*.

bake + **d** = bak**ed**

To add *–ed* to a word that ends in a consonant and a *–y*, change the *y* to *i* then add the suffix.

cry – **y** + **i** + **ed** = cr**ied**

Adding *–er*

To add *–er* as a suffix, add it to a base.

employ + **er** = employ**er**

To add *–er* to a word that has only one syllable and one short vowel sound, double the final consonant then add the suffix.

run + **n** + **er** = run**ner**

big + **g** + **er** = big**ger**

To add *–er* to a word that already ends in *–e*, do not add *–er*; add *–r*.

bake + **r** = bake**r**

Adding *–est*

To add *–est* as a suffix, add it to a base.

fast + **est** = fast**est**

To add *–est* to a word that has only one syllable and one short vowel sound, double the final consonant then add the suffix.

big + **g** + **est** = big**gest**

Adding *–full*

To add *–full* as a suffix to a base, take off one *l*.

help + **full** – **l** = help**ful**

wonder + **full** – **l** = wonder**ful**

Adding *–ing*

To add *–ing* as a suffix, add it to a base.

rest + **ing** = rest**ing**

employ + **ing** = employ**ing**

To add *–ing* to a word that ends in *–e*, take off the *e* then add the suffix.

bake – **e** + **ing** = bak**ing**

like – **e** + **ing** = lik**ing**

To add *–ing* to a word that has only one syllable and one short vowel sound, double the final consonant then add the suffix.

run + **n** + **ing** = run**ning**

clap + **p** + **ing** = clap**ping**

Adding -*ly*

To add –*ly* as a suffix, add it to a base.

dangerous + **ly** = dangerous**ly**

fearful + **ly** = fearful**ly**

To add –*ly* to a word that ends in –*y*, change the *y* to *i* then add the suffix.

happy – **y** + **i** + **ly** = happ**ily**

lazy – **y** + **i** + **ly** = laz**ily**

To add –*ly* to a word that ends in –*le*, take off the *le* then add the suffix.

simple – **le** + **ly** = simp**ly**

Adding -*ous*

To add –*ous* as a suffix to a word that ends in –*our*, change –*our* to –*or* then add the suffix.

humour – **u** + **ous** = humor**ous**

glamour – **u** + **ous** = glamor**ous**

Adding -*s*

To add an –*s* to a verb base, add it to the end of the word.

stay + **s** = stay**s**

employ + **s** = employ**s**

To add an –*s* to a verb that ends in a consonant and –*y*, change the *y* to *i* then add the suffix.

cry – **y** + **i** + **es** = cr**ies**

Other Spelling Conventions

Acronyms

An acronym is a word that is made by using the first letter of each word in a group of words. An acronym is used as a short way of referring to long names or common phrases. Also note that an initialism is similar to an acronym, but it consists of the initial letters pronounced separately (e.g. BBC). The following table lists some common acronyms and initialisms.

acronym	full version
Anzac	Australian and New Zealand Army Corps
ASAP	as soon as possible
DOB	date of birth
FAQ	frequently asked questions
FYI	for your information
NASA	National Aeronautics and Space Administration
radar	radio detection and ranging
sonar	sound navigation and ranging
T&C	terms and conditions
TAFE	Technical and Further Education
tba	to be announced
tbc	to be confirmed
WIP	work in progress

Some acronyms have become common as a result of communication via digital technology, e.g. in text messages.

acronym	full version
ATM	at the moment
BRB	be right back
CW	content warning
FOMO	fear of missing out
FWIW	for what it's worth

>>

acronym	full version
GOAT	**g**reatest **o**f **a**ll **t**ime
IDK	**I d**on't **k**now
IMHO	**i**n **m**y **h**onest (*or* **h**umble) **o**pinion
IMO	**i**n **m**y **o**pinion
IYKYK	**i**f **y**ou **k**now, **y**ou **k**now
LOL	**l**aughing (*or* **l**augh) **o**ut **l**oud
LMK	**l**et **m**e **k**now
NVM	**n**e**v**er **m**ind
OMG	**o**h **m**y **g**od
RN	**r**ight **n**ow
SMH	**s**haking (*or* **s**hake) **m**y **h**ead
TIL	**t**oday **I l**earned

Abbreviations

An abbreviation is a single word or phrase that has been shortened. Single words can have letters removed to make a contraction.

Abbreviations do not have a full stop when the last letter of the full word is also the last letter of the shortened form.

Abbreviations where the final letter of the full word is different from the final letter of the contracted form have a full stop after the abbreviations.

abbreviation	full word	abbreviation	full word
Rd	Road	Prof.	Professor
Dr	Doctor	Capt.	Captain
Pty	Proprietary	Co.	Company

Contractions

Contractions are phrases containing two words that have been combined into a single word. An apostrophe is used to indicate where a letter or letters have been left out.

words	*contraction*	*words*	*contraction*
are not	are**n't**	she is	she**'s**
can not	ca**n't**	should not	should**n't**
could not	could**n't**	that is	that**'s**
did not	did**n't**	they are	they**'re**
do not	do**n't**	they shall	they**'ll**
does not	does**n't**	they will	they**'ll**
has not	has**n't**	was not	was**n't**
have not	have**n't**	we are	we**'re**
he is	he**'s**	we shall	we**'ll**
I am	I**'m**	we will	we**'ll**
I shall	I**'ll**	will not	wo**n't**
I will	I**'ll**	you are	you**'re**
is not	is**n't**	you shall	you**'ll**
it is	it**'s**	you will	you**'ll**

4 Vocabulary and Word Lists

Building Vocabulary

The word *vocabulary* refers to the range of words a person uses when writing and speaking. Good writers try to use a variety of different words rather than just a limited selection, as this makes their writing more interesting. For example, the adjective *big* could be replaced by the following words:

bulky, enormous, extensive, gigantic, huge, immense, large, massive, significant, sizeable, substantial, vast

The verb *see* could be replaced by:

gaze, glance, glare, glimpse, look, peek, peep, peer, stare, watch

For more examples of alternative vocabulary, see Word List 1 on pages 57–66.

Students can build vocabulary in a few ways: learning about word bases, prefixes and suffixes (discussed in Spelling Generalisations on pages 44–8); reading books, watching visual content such as movies, television shows and videos; listening to podcasts; using different reference materials; researching information from different sources; and communicating with other people in a variety of situations.

When vocabulary is being discussed, it can be helpful to classify many words into the following groups.

Vocabulary Note

While students are expanding their vocabulary, it is important to note that some words are often mistakenly used. For example, *bought* and *brought* are often confused. For more examples of commonly misused words, see Word List 2 on pages 67–70.

Antonyms

Antonyms are words that are opposite in meaning.

day and **night**

careful and **careless**

comfortable and **uncomfortable**

Common prefixes for making antonyms are:

dis – **dis**appear, **dis**like, **dis**agree

il – **il**literate, **il**legible

im – **im**polite, **im**possible

in – **in**correct, **in**visible

mis – **mis**understand, **mis**taken

non – **non**sense, **non**stick

un – **un**happy, **un**finished

The most common suffix for making antonyms is:

less – harm**less**, care**less**

Compound words

Compound words are words made by joining two or more smaller words.

break + **fast** = **breakfast**

fire + **fighters** = **firefighters**

foot + **ball** = **football**

note + **book** = **notebook**

over + **seas** = **overseas**

pop + **corn** = **popcorn**

snow + **flake** = **snowflake**

sun + **flower** = **sunflower**

Homonyms

Homonyms are words that have the same spelling or the same sound, but have different meanings. Homophones and homographs are both examples of homonyms.

Luke taught me how to **cast** the fishing line.

Muhammad broke his arm playing football and had to wear a **cast** for six weeks.

Homographs

Homographs are words that have the same spelling, but mean different things and can be pronounced differently.

I had to **produce** my best apple pie to win the baking competition.

We purchased fresh **produce** at the markets stalls.

Homophones

Homophones are words that sound the same, but are spelt differently and have different meanings.

their, there, they're

blew, blue

hair, hare

For a list of common homophones, see Word List 3 on pages 71–82.

Portmanteau words

Portmanteau words are words that blend the sounds and combine the meanings of two other words.

biopic = **biography** + **picture**

bromance = **brother** + **romance**

email = **electronic** + **mail**

emoticons = **emotions** + **icons**

frenemy = **friend** + **enemy**

hangry = **hungry** + **angry**

malware = **malicious** + **software**

webinar = **web** + **seminar**

Synonyms

Synonyms are words that have a similar meaning.

afraid, frightened, scared

pale, faint, whitish

See pages 57–65 for Alternative Vocabulary choices for common words.

References for Spelling and Vocabulary

Dictionary

A printed dictionary contains an alphabetical list of words and their meanings. An online dictionary is a searchable database that can be browsed in alphabetical order or just by searching specific words. A dictionary can be used to:

- check the correct spelling of unknown or unfamiliar words
- check the pronunciation of words

  flick (*flik*)
- identify the function of a word in a sentence

  dry – *adjective*: without moisture; *verb*: to make or become dry
- locate the origin of some words

  cafe – a place that sells coffee (French: coffee)
- indicate some common prefixes and suffixes.

  makes, making, made

Thesaurus

A printed thesaurus is a list of words, often in alphabetical order, with their synonyms. An online thesaurus is a searchable database that can be browsed in alphabetical order or just by searching specific words. A thesaurus can be used to:

- find a more formal or informal word to suit the context of the writing

  beg – implore
- find a word with a more precise meaning

  looked – gazed, peered

- avoid repetition of a word that has already been used

  said – claimed, expressed, groaned, muttered, replied, shouted

- find a word with a slightly different meaning.

  operation – action, procedure

Spell check

Spell check is a language tool on computers that is used to check the spelling of typed words. This can be set as an automatic feature. Misspelt words are underlined with a wavy line, which notifies the writer to check the spelling. If the writer clicks on the underlined word, the spell check lists some possible words to replace the misspelt word. Sometimes, spell check is used by writers to specifically check the spelling in a section of a document, or throughout the whole document. Care must be taken using spell check in the following situations:

- when distinguishing between Australian/British and American spellings

  neighbour, neighbor

- when using homophones (often the wrong word is typed, but if it is spelt correctly, it will not be recognised as a mistake)

  I was **to** tired.

  I was **too** tired.

- when the incorrect word has been typed, but is spelt correctly.

  I **was** my neighbour's dog.

  I **saw** my neighbour's dog.

Writers should also use their knowledge of the way words look, how letter combinations are commonly used, prefixes and suffixes, and the origins of words to spell words correctly.

Word List 1: Alternative Vocabulary

Editing a text can include considering a more advanced or sophisticated choice of vocabulary. For many common words, there is a number of alternative words that can be used to enrich the writing or make it more formal. These words can also help to avoid repetition, intensify or modify the meaning, or distinguish between shades of meaning.

The following adjectives, nouns, adverbs and verbs can be used to make texts more specific to a particular audience or more accurate in their description of people, places or things. Note that not all words in each list are interchangeable; a dictionary or thesaurus can be used to clarify the meanings of selected words.

Alternative adjectives

able – capable, clever, competent, experienced, expert, gifted, practised, skilful, skilled, talented

alone – abandoned, apart, deserted, lonely, lonesome, unaccompanied, unaided, unassisted

angry – annoyed, cross, enraged, exasperated, fierce, fuming, furious, heated, ill-tempered, infuriated, irate, livid, outraged

awful – alarming, appalling, dire, distressing, dreadful, hideous, horrible, shocking, terrible, unpleasant

bad (or **mean**) – cruel, disobedient, evil, harmful, malicious, nasty, naughty, ruthless, villainous, wicked, wrong

beautiful – appealing, attractive, delightful, gorgeous, radiant, stunning

best – finest, foremost, outstanding, supreme, unsurpassed

big – bulky, burly, colossal, enormous, extensive, gigantic, huge, immense, large, massive, significant, sizeable, substantial, vast

brave – bold, courageous, daring, fearless, gallant, heroic, intrepid

bright – brilliant, illuminated, radiant, shining, sparkling, twinkling, vivid

>>

brown – bronze, chestnut, chocolate, coffee, hazel, tan, tanned, toasted

calm – mild, peaceful, placid, restful, serene, smooth, still, tranquil

careful – accurate, attentive, cautious, conscientious, particular, precise, thoughtful, wary, watchful

certain – assured, confident, convinced, positive, sure

clear – bright, cloudless, distinct, explicit, express, fine, obvious, sunny, unclouded

clever – astute, capable, gifted, ingenious, innovative, intelligent, knowing, sensible, shrewd, skilful, smart, talented

cold – bitter, bleak, chilly, freezing, frosty, frozen, icy, wintry

dark – cloudy, dim, murky, overcast, pitch-black, shadowy, unlit

dirty – filthy, grimy, grubby, muddy, polluted, soiled, unclean

dry – arid, barren, dehydrated, parched, thirsty, waterless

eerie – frightening, ghostly, mysterious, strange, unearthly, weird

empty – blank, deserted, hollow, uninhabited, unoccupied, vacant, void

fast – hasty, hurried, quick, rapid, speedy, swift

fierce – brutal, cruel, dangerous, ferocious, savage, threatening, untamed, vicious, wild

frightened – afraid, alarmed, panicky, petrified, scared, startled, terrified, terrorised, unnerved

funny – absurd, amusing, comical, entertaining, hilarious, humorous, laughable, ludicrous, peculiar, strange, unusual, weird, witty

gentle – humane, kind, meek, peaceful, placid, serene

good – accomplished, admirable, decent, delightful, enjoyable, excellent, fine, first-class, high-quality, moral, noble, pleasant, praiseworthy, superior, virtuous, worthy

>>

great – excellent, impressive, majestic, notable, proficient, remarkable, skilful, talented

happy – blissful, cheerful, cheery, content, delighted, ecstatic, elated, excited, exultant, glad, jovial, joyful, jubilant, overjoyed, pleased, thrilled

hard – complex, complicated, difficult, exhausting, firm, intricate, involved, perplexing, puzzling, solid, tough, wearying

hot – boiling, burning, flaming, heated, scalding, scorching, searing, sweltering

kind – affectionate, considerate, courteous, friendly, generous, gentle, obliging, thoughtful

like – approximating, comparable, equivalent, identical, resembling, similar

lonely – abandoned, alone, apart, solitary

lots of (or **many**) – abundance, countless, limitless, numerous, profuse, several, various

loud – blaring, boisterous, deafening, noisy, piercing, raucous, riotous, rowdy, shrill, strident, thunderous

many – *see* **lots of**

marvellous – amazing, astounding, breathtaking, extraordinary, miraculous, remarkable, wondrous

mean – *see* **bad**

neat – orderly, systematic, tidy

new – current, fresh, latest, modern, recent, up-to-date

nice – agreeable, amiable, attractive, cheery, courteous, fine, friendly, good, kind, likeable, lovely, pleasant, pleasurable, polite, well-mannered

old – aged, ancient, antiquated, antique, elderly, mature, original, primitive, senior, vintage

pleased – contented, delighted, euphoric, glad, gratified, happy, pleased, satisfied, thrilled

>>

red – cherry, crimson, rose, ruby, scarlet

rich – abundant, affluent, ample, copious, fruitful, wealthy

sad – depressed, dismal, doleful, glum, mournful, unhappy

sharp – acute, jagged, pointed, serrated

sleek – glossy, lustrous, shiny, smooth

slow – dawdling, gradual, leisurely, measured, unhurried

small – diminutive, insignificant, insufficient, little, meagre, miniature, minute, petite, tiny, trivial

soft – cushioned, pliable, spongy, squashy, supple

sore – inflamed, irritated, painful, sensitive, tender

strong – muscular, powerful, robust, sturdy, tough

sure – certain, clear, confident, convinced, definite, positive

terrible – appalling, awful, dire, dreadful, frightful, ghastly, gruesome, hideous, horrendous, horrible, horrifying, revolting, shocking

tired – drained, drowsy, exhausted, fatigued, sleepy, spent, weary

weak – delicate, exhausted, faint, feeble, fragile, frail, spent

wet – damp, dank, dripping, moist, saturated, sodden, soggy

wonderful – amazing, astonishing, astounding, breathtaking, brilliant, excellent, fantastic, magnificent, miraculous, outstanding, remarkable, sensational, superb, terrific, tremendous

worn – frayed, ragged, shabby, tattered, threadbare

worried – afraid, anxious, bothered, concerned, distressed, fearful, frightened, nervous, scared, tense, tormented, troubled, uneasy, upset

Alternative verbs

ache – hurt, pain, throb, twinge

achieve – accomplish, attain, complete, effect, execute, finish, fulfil, obtain, reach

admire – adore, appreciate, idolise, praise, respect, worship

alarm – distress, frighten, panic, scare, startle, terrify, terrorise

amaze – astonish, astound, bewilder, startle, stun, stupefy, surprise

appear – come across as, give the impression of, seem

argue – disagree, quarrel, squabble, wrangle

ask – beg, implore, inquire, invite, plead, query, question, quiz

begin – commence, initiate, instigate, start

bite – chew, crunch, crush, gnaw, nibble

build – assemble, construct, erect, establish, fabricate

climb – ascend, clamber, mount, rise, scale

complain – groan, grumble, moan, wail, whine

creep – crawl, slither, squirm, worm, wriggle, writhe

cry – blubber, sob, wail, weep, whimper

disagree – conflict, contest, contradict, deviate, differ, dispute, diverge, object, oppose, quarrel

do – accomplish, achieve, complete, create, perform, produce

drink – gulp, guzzle, sip, swallow

eat – chew, consume, devour, munch, swallow

>>

explain – clarify, define, demonstrate, describe, interpret, resolve, solve, teach

fall – cascade, collapse, crash, descend, pitch, plummet, plunge, settle, sink, stumble, topple, trip, tumble

feel – caress, finger, manipulate, maul, paw, stroke, touch

find – discover, encounter, locate, recognise, retrieve, uncover, unearth

gather – accumulate, amass, assemble, collect, congregate, hoard, muster, round up, stockpile

get – achieve, acquire, attain, become, catch, find, grasp, grow, obtain, receive, understand

go – amble, depart, drive, leave, proceed, run, saunter, stroll, travel, walk

help – aid, assist, cooperate, support

hold – clutch, cradle, embrace, grasp, grip, have, keep, maintain

hope – anticipate, aspire, believe, desire, trust

hurry – accelerate, dash, hasten, hustle, quicken, run, rush, scurry

increase – amplify, boost, develop, enhance, escalate, expand, extend, intensify, magnify, multiply, swell

laugh – chortle, chuckle, giggle, snigger

let – allow, authorise, permit, sanction

like – admire, adore, appreciate, enjoy, love, prefer, relish, resemble

look – consider, contemplate, eye, gape, gaze, glance, glare, glimpse, inspect, observe, peep, scan, scrutinise, study, survey, view, watch

love – cherish, idolise, relish, treasure

make – appoint, assemble, bake, become, brew, build, compel, compose, concoct, construct, craft, create, earn, effect, establish, formulate, generate, manufacture, produce

>>

move – advance, march, proceed, progress, relocate, transfer, transport

push – boost, drive, elbow, encourage, force, induce, jostle, move forward, persuade, press, promote, ram, shoulder, shove, thrust, urge

read – peruse, scan, study

run – bolt, career, dart, dash, hasten, scamper, scramble, scurry, sprint

say – add, affirm, agree, allege, announce, ask, cry, declare, divulge, maintain, mention, mumble, murmur, mutter, pronounce, repeat, reply, respond, reveal, speak, state, suggest, suppose, tell, think, utter, whisper

see – gaze, glance, glare, glimpse, identify, look, notice, observe, peek, peep, peer, recognise, sight, spot, stare, view, watch, witness

shout – bark, bawl, bellow, call, holler, roar, scream, screech, yell

spin – pirouette, revolve, rotate, turn, twirl, whirl

take – acquire, clutch, receive, secure, seize, trap

talk – chatter, confer, converse, gossip, speak, utter

tell – announce, communicate, disclose, express, inform, mention, reveal, state, utter

think – anticipate, assume, believe, conclude, consider, deem, deliberate, envisage, estimate, expect, feel, imagine, judge, know, ponder, reason, recall, recollect, reflect, regard, remember, sense, suppose, understand, weigh up

try – aim, attempt, endeavour, strive, struggle, undertake

understand – appreciate, comprehend, fathom, know, realise

use – employ, operate, practise

walk – amble, hike, march, pace, saunter, stagger, step, stride, stroll, toddle, tramp, tread, trudge

whine – cry, grumble, moan, wail

yell – bawl, howl, scream, screech, shout, shriek, squeal

Alternative adverbs

aloud – audibly, clearly, distinctly, plainly

also – additionally, as well as, besides, furthermore, in addition, including, plus, what's more

always – consistently, continually, forever, perpetually, repeatedly

easily – comfortably, effortlessly, simply, smoothly

now – immediately, instantly, promptly, straightaway

quickly – abruptly, briskly, fast, hastily, hurriedly, promptly, rapidly, speedily, swiftly

quietly – inaudibly, noiselessly, silently, softly

really – actually, certainly, genuinely, indeed, positively, surely, truly

then – after that, afterwards, following, later, meanwhile, next, subsequently

usually – commonly, generally, mainly, mostly, normally, ordinarily, regularly, routinely

very – awfully, deeply, enormously, especially, exceedingly, exceptionally, extraordinarily, extremely, fantastically, greatly, incredibly, remarkably, truly

Alternative nouns

accident – collision, crash, disaster, misadventure, misfortune, mishap

action – accomplishment, feat, operation, performance, proceeding, undertaking

air – atmosphere, blast, breath, breeze, draught, puff, waft, whiff, wind

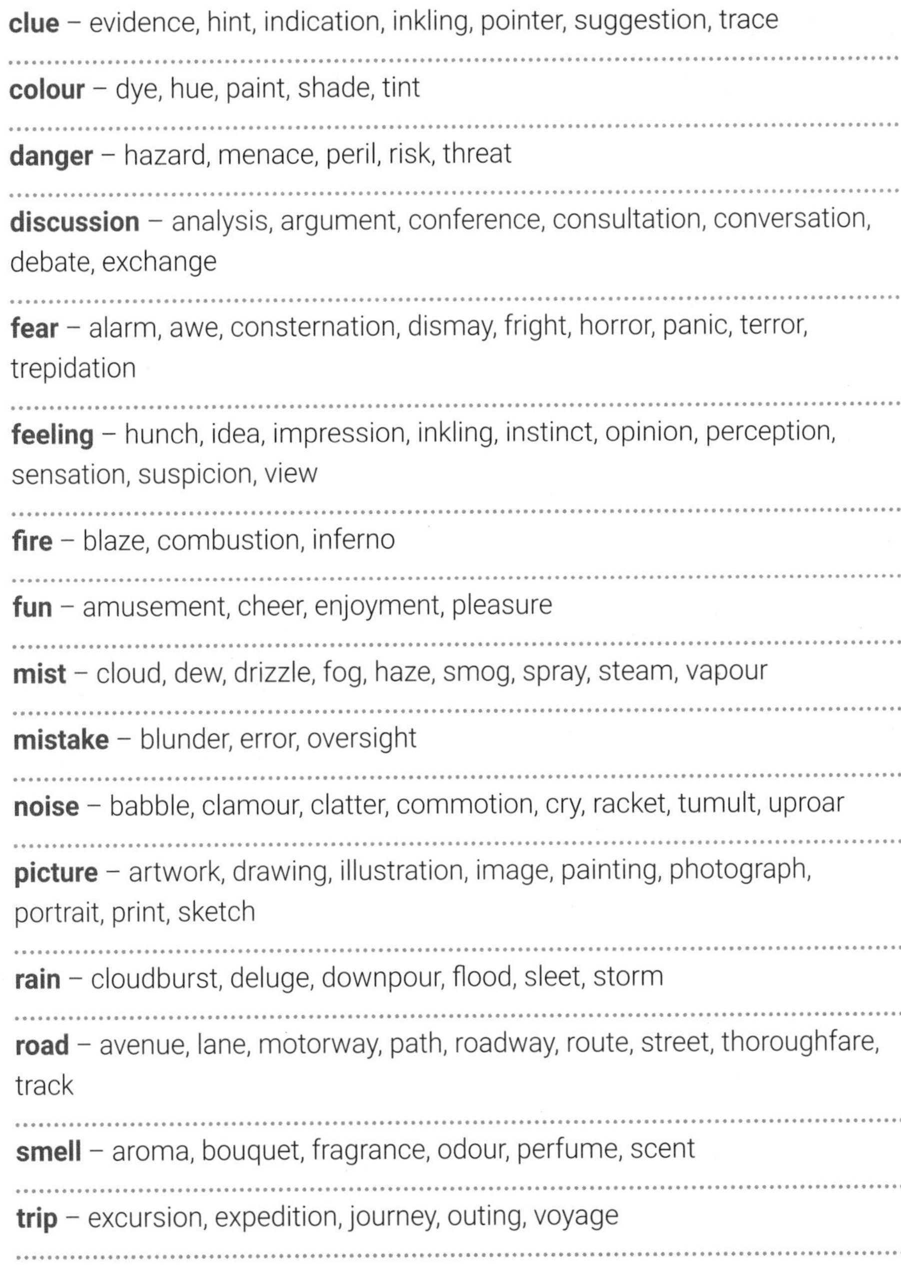

clue – evidence, hint, indication, inkling, pointer, suggestion, trace

colour – dye, hue, paint, shade, tint

danger – hazard, menace, peril, risk, threat

discussion – analysis, argument, conference, consultation, conversation, debate, exchange

fear – alarm, awe, consternation, dismay, fright, horror, panic, terror, trepidation

feeling – hunch, idea, impression, inkling, instinct, opinion, perception, sensation, suspicion, view

fire – blaze, combustion, inferno

fun – amusement, cheer, enjoyment, pleasure

mist – cloud, dew, drizzle, fog, haze, smog, spray, steam, vapour

mistake – blunder, error, oversight

noise – babble, clamour, clatter, commotion, cry, racket, tumult, uproar

picture – artwork, drawing, illustration, image, painting, photograph, portrait, print, sketch

rain – cloudburst, deluge, downpour, flood, sleet, storm

road – avenue, lane, motorway, path, roadway, route, street, thoroughfare, track

smell – aroma, bouquet, fragrance, odour, perfume, scent

trip – excursion, expedition, journey, outing, voyage

Collective nouns

Collective nouns are a type of common noun. They name groups of people, animals and things.

Examples of collective nouns for people are:

an army of soldiers	a choir of singers	a gang of thieves
a band of musicians	a circle of friends	a staff of workers
a board of directors	a class of students	a team of players
a body of students	a crew of workers on a ship	a troupe of dancers

Examples of collective nouns for animals are:

a clowder of cats	a herd of buffalo	a plague of insects
a colony of bats	a herd of cattle	a prickle of porcupines
a down of hares	a kindle of kittens	a sloth of bears
a flight of swallows	a litter of pups	a smack of jellyfish
a flock of birds	a murder of crows	a string of horses
a flock of sheep	a nest of rabbits	a team of oxen
a gaggle of geese	a paddle of platypuses	a tribe of goats
a herd of antelopes	a parliament of owls	a watch of nightingales

Examples of collective nouns for objects are:

a bouquet of flowers	a cluster of diamonds	a fleet of vehicles
a bunch of grapes	a clutch of eggs	a flight of stairs
a bunch (or hand) of bananas	a galaxy (or cluster) of stars	a punnet of strawberries
a chest of drawers	a library of books	a tuft of grass

Word List 2: Commonly Misused Words

Sometimes, two words sound almost the same and can easily be confused. Take care using these words when writing.

accept and **except**

accept – *verb;* to take or receive something; to consider something to be true; to agree in principle

I was asked to **accept** the trophy on behalf of the entire team.

except – *preposition*; other than; apart from; not including

All the puppies were tan, **except** one that had a black patch over its eye.

advice and **advise**

advice – *noun*; helpful information; a recommended course of action

Ms Wu gave me **advice** about how to prepare for my interview.

advise – *verb*; to inform or offer advice to someone

The teacher prepared a note to **advise** us of what we needed to take.

affect and **effect**

affect – *verb*; to cause or bring about change; to influence

The dumping of waste materials can severely **affect** the environment.

effect – *noun*; an outcome or result of change

The **effect** of the rain was to promote new growth in the local gardens.

effect – *verb*; to bring about; accomplish

In order to **effect** the change, the government had to increase taxes.

>>

among and **between**

among – *preposition*; in the midst of; expressing a relationship concerning three or more things

Sriharsha shared the sweets **among** all the children in the class.

between – *preposition*; a link or comparison of two things

Charul divided the seed **between** her two birds.

assure, ensure and **insure**

assure – *verb*; to convince or state positively

I **assure** you that your car will be safe here.

ensure – *verb*; to make certain, or guarantee

Quang put new batteries in the toys to **ensure** they would work properly.

insure – *verb*; to protect financially against loss or damage

The owner decided to **insure** the sports car for its purchase price.

bought and **brought**

bought – *verb*; past tense of *buy*

Amelia **bought** fresh bread at the bakery.

brought – *verb*; past tense of *bring*

Deepak **brought** a friend home at lunch time.

can and **may**

can – *verb* or *part of compound verb*; is able to; capable of

I **can** count to one hundred by fives.

may – *verb*; is allowed to; has permission

You **may** go on the school excursion on Thursday.

>>

choose and **chose**

choose – *verb*; to select from a list or group of alternatives

Alexander was allowed to **choose** a new pair of shoes.

chose – *verb*; past tense of *choose*

Yesterday, Alexander **chose** a new pair of shoes.

desert and **dessert**

desert – *noun*; an area of land covered with sand or ice, and having little or sparse vegetation due to low rainfall

An oasis is a fertile place in a **desert**.

desert – *verb*; to abandon a person or place without intent to return

"I'm sure Sooty would not **desert** her kittens," soothed Dad.

dessert – *noun*; the sweet course usually eaten at the end of a meal

After the roast lamb, we had caramel tart for **dessert**.

device and **devise**

device – *noun*; a plan, method or tool used to assist in completing a task

Mr Nguyen had a clever **device** for lifting the engine out of the truck.

devise – *verb*; to create, invent or plot

I had to **devise** a formula to solve the mathematical problem.

good and **well**

good – *adjective*; pleasing, well-behaved or of some benefit

It is a **good** idea to brush your teeth after each meal.

well – *adjective*; in good health

Having had a cold for several days, I was not feeling **well**.

well – *adverb*; properly, skilfully or carefully

The couple performed the dance extremely **well**.

well – *noun*; a hole in the ground from which water can be lifted to the surface

The bucket was used to lift water from the **well**.

>>

loose and lose

loose – *adjective*; not tight

My shoes were quite **loose**, as they were a size too big.

lose – *verb*; to misplace, or to be unable to find

Put your money safely in your pocket so you don't **lose** it.

of and off

of – *preposition*; belonging to, or coming from

The colour **of** the leaves changed from green to yellow during autumn.

off – *preposition*; no longer attached to or associated with; away from

We turned **off** the highway at a major intersection.

off – *adverb*; to deactivate or disengage

"Your hat should be taken **off** when you come inside," reminded Mum.

quiet and quite

quiet – *adjective*; not making much noise; serene or tranquil

Once the storyteller started reading, all the children became **quiet**.

quite – *adverb* (*intensifier*); partially or absolutely

"I was **quite** surprised when you turned up!" exclaimed Ahmed.

scared and scarred

scared – *verb*; past tense of *scare*; to frighten or alarm

James **scared** his brother by banging loudly on the front door.

scared – *adjective*; frightened or alarmed by someone or something

I was **scared** during the storm, so I hid under the blankets until it had passed.

scarred – *adjective*; marked by the healing of a wound

The **scarred** remains of the rainforest were evidence of the fierce bushfires.

scarred – *verb*; past tense of *scar*; to mark or become marked with a scar

My arm was slightly **scarred** after I had chicken pox.

Word List 3: Homophones

Homophones are words that have the same sound, but different meanings and spellings. It is important in written texts that the correct word is used.

allowed and **aloud**

allowed – *verb*; past tense of *allow*; to have or to give permission to do something

Dankila was **allowed** to spend the night at his friend's house.

aloud – *adverb*; not silently; in a spoken or natural voice

I read the newspaper article **aloud** to my family.

awe, oar, or and **ore**

awe – *noun*; wonder or dread

I watched in **awe** as the spacecraft landed on Mars.

oar – *noun*; a paddle used for rowing a boat

The **oar** got stuck on the bottom of the river.

or – *conjunction*; an alternative

You may choose the red **or** the green shirt.

ore – *noun*; a rock or mineral from which metals can be extracted

Iron **ore** is mined in Western Australia.

bare and **bear**

bare – *adjective*; unclothed or without covering

After the fight, the dog had a **bare** patch on its leg.

bear – *verb*; to support or hold up

When we moved the old table, I had to **bear** most of its weight.

bear – *noun;* a large mammal

From the bus, we saw a grizzly **bear** in the distance.

bean and been

bean – *noun*; a vegetable

Dad cooked **beans** with chilli for dinner last night.

been – *verb*; a form of the verb *be*

I have **been** practising the drums every day.

blew and blue

blew – *verb*; past tense of *blow*

The wind **blew** the leaves along the street.

blue – *adjective*; a colour

When the storm cleared, the sky was **blue** again.

brake and break

brake – *noun*; a device for slowing down or stopping a vehicle

As I sped down the hill on the old bike, I realised it didn't have a **brake**!

brake – *verb*; to cause something to slow down or stop moving

You will need to **brake** to go around the corner safely.

break – *noun*; a crack, or the place where something becomes fractured

The **break** in my arm meant I had to wear a plaster cast for several weeks.

break – *noun*; a rest or holiday

After we had a short **break**, we returned to our homework.

break – *verb*; to snap or separate into pieces

Be careful with the plate – if you drop it, it could **break**.

coarse and course

coarse – *adjective*; rough, not smooth

I used **coarse** sandpaper to rub back the paintwork.

course – *noun*; a series of lessons in a particular area of learning; the path of a river

Eswari enrolled in a scrap-booking **course** on the weekends.

>>

currant and **current**

currant – *noun*; a small, dried grape

Many people put **currants** in a fruitcake.

current – *noun*; a steady flow of water, air or electricity

We floated downstream with the **current**.

current – *adjective*; in the immediate present; happening now

Our school featured in the **current** events program on television.

drawers and **draws**

drawers – *noun*; an open section of a cabinet that slides in and out, used for storing a variety of items

The saucepans were stored in the kitchen **drawers**.

draws – *verb*; present tense of *draw*; to sketch with a pen or pencil

The artist **draws** in pencil before applying the paint.

draws – *verb*; present tense of *draw*; to drag or pull steadily

The farmer **draws** water from the well to fill the troughs each evening.

flour and **flower**

flour – *noun*; a powder resulting from grinding grain

Sift the **flour** into the bowl with the creamed butter and sugar.

flower – *noun*; the part of a plant that is usually brightly coloured

The bride had beautiful pink **flowers** in her bouquet.

foreword and **forward**

foreword – *noun*; an introductory statement at the beginning of a book

I read the **foreword** to learn how the book was researched.

forward – *adjective*; directed or moving ahead; at, in or near the front

The player who made a **forward** pass was penalised.

forward – *adverb*; towards or at a place ahead, in space or time

The race car charged **forward** when the green flag was dropped.

>>

fort and **fought**

fort – *noun*; a protected enclosure or building

The guards surrounded the **fort** to prevent attack by the enemy.

fought – *verb*; past tense of *fight*

I **fought** my way into the open space, gasping for breath.

groan and **grown**

groan – *noun*; a sound signifying pain or disapproval

The animal's **groan** could be heard a long distance away.

groan – *verb*; to make a sound signifying pain or disapproval

I heard the animal **groan** as it struggled to escape the trap.

grown – *adjective*; developed or matured

Only a fully **grown** man could reach the top of the cupboard.

grown – *verb*; a form of the verb *grow*; to become bigger or taller

My dress is too short because I have **grown** since last summer.

guessed and **guest**

guessed – *verb*; past tense of *guess*; to estimate

I **guessed** he was about ten years old.

guest – *noun*; a person invited to a place or event, to be entertained or offered hospitality

My family cooked dinner for a special **guest** on Friday evening.

hair and **hare**

hair – *noun*; threadlike growth on the skin of mammals

I washed my **hair** when I came home from the swimming pool.

hare – *noun*; a mammal, larger than a rabbit, with long ears and legs

The **Hare** *and the Tortoise* is a well-known fable.

>>

hoarse and horse

hoarse – *adjective*; having a husky voice

After cheering for my favourite team, my voice was **hoarse**.

horse – *noun*; a four-legged animal used for pulling a cart or riding

We exercised the **horse** by riding it around the paddock.

its and it's

its – *determiner*; belonging to, or associated with

The baby smiled when I looked in **its** pram.

it's – the contracted form of *it is* and *it has*

It's going to be very cold tonight.

It's happened again.

knew and new

knew – *verb*; past tense of *know*; to understand or to feel certain about

"I **knew** you were going to win!" said Maali.

new – *adjective*; fresh; recently made; not old

My parents bought me a **new** outfit to wear to the concert.

pain and pane

pain – *noun*; physical hurt; discomfort caused by sickness or injury

Oliver's sharp **pain** was suspected to be appendicitis.

pane – *noun*; a sheet of glass

Tuan cleaned the window **pane** with newspaper.

pair and pear

pair – *noun*; a set of two similar things

I found a **pair** of black socks in my drawer.

pear – *noun*; a type of fruit

I enjoy a **pear** with cheese for a snack.

>>

passed and past

passed – *verb*; past tense of *pass*

When I **passed** Grandpa in the street, I stopped to help carry his parcels.

past – *noun*; a time before the present

We talked about the people who lived there in the **past**.

past – *preposition*; beyond

The winner will be the first one **past** the post.

past – *adverb*; tells where

We pulled over to the side of the road to let the truck go **past**.

peace and piece

peace – *noun*; a state of harmony; absence of war

Peace was declared in 1945.

piece – *noun*; a section or portion of something

I thoroughly enjoyed the large **piece** of lemon meringue pie.

practice and practise

practice – *noun*; a rehearsal

The students went to choir **practice** after school.

practise – *verb*; to perform an action repeatedly to improve the skill level

My piano teacher told me to **practise** the scales every day.

principal and principle

principal – *noun*; the head of a school, college or educational institution

The **principal** at our school has a kind but firm approach with all students.

principle – *noun*; a basic value that provides a system of belief or behaviour

Being punctual is a good **principle** to follow.

raw and **roar**

raw – *adjective*; uncooked

I ate **raw** carrot in my salad.

roar – *noun*; a loud, growling sound

In the distance, Charlotte heard the lion's **roar**.

roar – *verb*; to make a loud, growling sound

"The lion will **roar** if you go too near the cage!" warned the keeper.

road and **rode**

road – *noun*; a street for vehicles to travel on

"Slow down when the **road** is wet," advised the driving instructor.

rode – *verb*; past tense of *ride*

When we **rode** our bikes, we always put on our helmets.

sauce and **source**

sauce – *noun*; a liquid mixed with or poured on to food to add flavour

Thi stirred the **sauce** with a wooden spoon.

source – *noun*; the point, person or place where something comes from

The **source** of the trouble was their disagreement about recycling.

saw, **soar** and **sore**

saw – *noun*; a tool with a metal blade, used for cutting

A builder uses a hammer and a **saw**.

saw – *verb*; past tense of *see*

I **saw** my reflection in the water at the edge of the stream.

soar – *verb*; to rise or fly into the air

We watched the birds **soar** among the treetops.

sore – *noun*; a painful wound or injury

Lucas had a **sore** on his leg from where he tripped and fell.

sore – *adjective*; sensitive to pain; tender

My throat was **sore** and my head was aching.

>>

scene and **seen**

scene – *noun*; the place where an action or event occurs

Suddenly, police cars arrived at the **scene** of the crime.

seen – *verb*; a form of the verb *see*

"Have you **seen** Ms Overton?" asked Disha.

seam and **seem**

seam – *noun*; the line along which two edges are joined

I quickly sewed the **seam** so she could adjust the garment.

seem – *verb*; to appear to be; to give the impression

I **seem** confident, but most of the time I'm nervous.

seas, **sees** and **seize**

seas – *noun*; plural form of *sea;* a great body of salt water

The **seas** were rough when we first set sail.

sees – *verb*; present tense of *see*

If anyone **sees** my lost lunch box, please let me know.

seize – *verb*; to grab or take hold of

I will **seize** this opportunity to tell you my idea.

sight and **site**

sight – *noun*; vision; the power of seeing

When my **sight** deteriorated, I decided it was time to wear glasses.

site – *noun*; the piece of land where something is to be placed or constructed

The bulldozer rumbled onto the building **site**.

>>

their, there and they're

their – *possessive pronoun* and *determiner*; referring to or associated with *them*

The children tidied **their** rooms on Sunday.

there – *adverb*; at, in or to a particular place or position

Please put your bags over **there** near the wall.

they're – the contracted form of *they are*

All the children are excited because **they're** going to the circus tonight.

tire and tyre

tire – *verb*; to lose energy or become weary

After hiking for three hours, the party of bushwalkers began to **tire**.

tyre – *noun*; an inflated rubber ring placed over the rim of a wheel

The mechanic checked that the spare **tyre** was inflated properly.

to, too and two

to – *preposition*; towards

Ismail went for a run up **to** the top of the hill.

too – *adverb*; also, as well as, extremely

It was **too** hot talking while standing in the sun.

two – *determiner*; the number two

When my sister was **two** years old, we moved to live in the city.

toe and tow

toe – *noun*; one of the digits on the foot

Medika kicked her **toe** on the corner of the cupboard.

tow – *verb*; to pull or drag using a rope, chain or cable

When Noah's car broke down, he had to **tow** it to the garage to be repaired.

>>

waist and **waste**

waist – *noun*; the part of the body between the ribs and the hips

"Tie the rope around your **waist**," yelled the rescuer, "and I'll pull you out!"

waste – *noun*; anything unused, or not used to potential

Do not leave your **waste** beside the road.

waste – *verb*; to use or expend carelessly

"If you **waste** time, you will be late for the movie," called Nur.

wait and **weight**

wait – *verb*; to remain in place until an expected event

"Please **wait** here," said the shop assistant. "I won't be long."

weight – *noun*; the heaviness of an object

I put the fish on the scales to check its **weight**.

war and **wore**

war – *noun*; armed conflict between two or more groups or nations

Troops were deployed to the **war** overseas.

wore – *verb*; past tense of *wear*

Anika **wore** an evening gown to the ball.

ware, wear, we're and **where**

ware – *noun*; any manufactured item that is for sale

The old lady sat by the fountain, hoping to sell her **wares** to passers-by.

wear – *verb*; to carry something on your body as clothing or jewellery

All members of the team had to **wear** their uniforms.

we're – the contracted form of *we are*

"**We're** going to the beach for our holiday," I said.

where – *adverb*; in, at or to what place

"Please put the books **where** they won't get wet," requested the librarian.

way, **weigh** and **whey**

way – *noun*; a manner or method of doing something

"I like the confident **way** you expressed your opinion," said the teacher.

way – *noun*; a route or direction

"Which **way** do you travel to the Harbour Bridge?" inquired the tourist.

weigh – *verb*; to measure how heavy something is

The butcher had to **weigh** the meat to calculate the price.

whey – *noun*; the watery part of curdled milk

During the cheese-making process, the curd is separated from the **whey**.

weak and **week**

weak – *adjective*; not strong

"You are too **weak** to lift weights," scoffed James.

week – *noun*; a period of time equal to seven days

Our house was painted last **week**.

weather, **wether** and **whether**

weather – *noun*; the state of the atmosphere (the temperature, humidity, wind and rainfall) at a particular place and time

If the **weather** is fine, we will go to the beach.

weather – *verb*; wear away or change the appearance of something by exposure to the atmosphere

The **weathered** exterior made the house look like it had been abandoned.

wether – *noun*; a castrated male sheep or goat

The **wethers** were separated from the rest of the flock.

whether – *conjunction*; expressing doubt or choice between alternatives

Kobe was undecided about **whether** to go to the party or stay at home.

which and witch

which – *pronoun*; a word used to begin a question or join clauses in a sentence

"**Which** hat is yours?" asked Chloe.

witch – *noun*; a person who practises magic or sorcery

Some fairy tales have a **witch** as one of the characters.

who's and whose

who's – the contracted form of *who is* and *who has*

"I wonder **who's** going to win this race?" said Ava.

"**Who's** ordered their lunch today?" said the teacher.

whose – *pronoun*; meaning *belonging to who* or *of who*

Chandika is a girl **whose** self-esteem is very high.

your and you're

your – *possessive pronoun* and *determiner*; of, associated with, or belonging to you

"Where are **your** swimmers?" quizzed the coach.

you're – the contracted form of *you are*

"**You're** so messy, Ngarra!" grumbled his sister.

5 Text Types

What Are Text Types?

Text types are pieces of writing that are created for a specific purpose and audience. Each text type contains a typical structure and some characteristic language features. When writers have the right knowledge and skills, they can create a range of literary and factual texts. There are different ways to express and organise information using a range of text types, and a variety of sentence structures and language features.

The writing process involves planning, drafting, revising and editing, and publishing stages.

Planning involves thinking about the purpose for writing and recognising the audience. Authors need to think carefully about what to write, clarify the topic and gather information. It is helpful to draw pictures, and write down key words, phrases or topic sentences to use.

Drafting is the first attempt at constructing the text. Authors refer to their planning notes as they write, and use the correct structure and language features of the selected text type.

Revising and editing Revising allows authors to reflect on what has been written. Receiving feedback from others and, if necessary, making changes to the language used can help to clarify ideas in the text. Editing involves proofreading and checking spelling, grammar and punctuation.

Publishing is the final stage of putting the completed text into a format suitable for the audience.

Recount

A Recount is a factual text. The **purpose** of a Recount is to retell and evaluate events and experiences.

Recount texts are written in past tense, because the events being retold have already taken place. A Recount includes an evaluation of the events that took place, explaining why the author enjoyed or didn't enjoy the experience.

The **audience** for a Recount text can vary, and may depend on the topic of the Recount. A simple email to a friend or relative may be a retelling of a family event or activity the writer attended. If the writer attended a music concert, an email written to their music teacher at school could explain how the student enjoyed the performance.

Text structure

Title

- The title relates to the events or experiences being retold.

Orientation

- The orientation provides information about *who, when, where* and *why*.

Sequence of Events

- The events are presented in chronological order.
- The events or experiences are organised in paragraphs.
- Time and sequence words help to sequence the paragraphs.
- Each paragraph begins with a topic sentence.
- Each paragraph includes supporting information that adds description and detail.

Personal Comment

- The personal comment evaluates the events that took place.

The following text models the appropriate structure for a Recount.

A Special Day

To : Lola_F@penpals.com

Dear Lola,

Yesterday was a special day. It was the end of Ramadan. We had lunch at my cousin's house to celebrate Eid ul-Fitr.

First, we all put on our best clothes. I wore a new shirt. My sister wore a new dress.

Then, we walked around the corner to my cousin Zara's house. Zara's house was decorated with lights.

Next, I helped set the tables for lunch. My whole family was there, so one table was not big enough!

After that, it was time to eat. My sister wanted to eat dessert, but Mum asked her to eat some meat, rice and vegetables first.

I love Eid ul-Fitr.

From,

Amir

Language features

In this Recount, the following examples of language features (refer to pages 2–19) have been included:

language feature	*examples*
nouns	day, lunch, clothes, sister, corner, family, table, vegetables
proper nouns	Lola, Ramadan, Eid ul-Fitr, Mum, Amir
noun groups	cousin's house, Zara's house

>>

language feature	*examples*
adjectives	special, best, new, whole
past-tense relating verbs	was, had
past-tense action verbs	wore, walked, helped, wanted, asked
adverbs	on, there, first
time and sequence words	yesterday, first, next, after that
prepositional phrases	at my cousin's house, around the corner

Sentences

The following sentence types (refer to pages 19–21) have also been included:

sentence type	*examples*
simple sentence	Yesterday was a special day.
compound sentence	My sister wanted to eat dessert, but Mum asked her to eat some meat, rice and vegetables first.
complex sentence	My whole family was there, so one table was not big enough!

Recount Note

Reported speech is used in the writing of Recount texts.

Language effects

Some figurative language (refer to pages 26–31), such as similes, can be used in Recount texts. Evaluative language (refer to page 31) that expresses how the author felt about the experience is generally included in the personal comment, but may also be scattered throughout the text.

Vocabulary

When revising and editing a text, the writer can consider a more advanced or sophisticated choice of words (refer to pages 52–82).

In this text, the word *walked* could be replaced with *strolled*.

Text forms

A Recount can be written in the form of:

- a journal or diary entry
- a letter or email
- a personal or factual recount
- a newspaper article
- a school newsletter article
- a social media post or video
- a timeline.

Description

A Description is an informative text. The **purpose** of a Description is to describe the characteristics of a particular person, place or thing.

Description texts are written in present tense, unless they describe a person, place or thing that no longer exists, when it can then be written in past tense. A Description includes an evaluation that has a personal comment about the subject.

The **audience** for a Description text can vary, and may depend on what is being described. A Description of an animal may appeal to children who would like a new pet. A Description about a sporting hero may be of particular interest to a person who plays the same sport.

Text structure

Title

- The title is concise and identifies the subject being described.

Introduction

- The introduction informs readers about the subject being described. The subject is a particular person, place or thing.

Characteristics

- The characteristics describe details about the subject.
- They describe what the person looks like, what the person does and special features of the person. They describe what the place looks like, what it is used for and other interesting information about the place. They describe where the thing is found, what it looks like, what it does and other special features it has.
- Information is grouped in paragraphs.
- Each paragraph begins with a topic sentence.
- Each paragraph includes supporting information that adds detail.

Evaluation

- The evaluation provides a personal comment about the subject.

The following text models the appropriate structure for a Description.

A City Market

Big markets are found in many cities around the world. Many people visit the markets to buy fresh food and other goods.

This market has hundreds of stalls. It has been held in the same place for many years. Cheese and other dairy foods are sold in one part of the market. Meat and fish stalls are in a different area. Fresh fruit and vegetables are found in another part of the market, too. There are also stalls that sell toys, clothes and lots of other goods.

On market days, crowds of shoppers walk around buying the things they need. Market stall owners call out the prices of their goods in cheerful voices. Some shoppers stop to buy lunch or a snack.

I always like to visit the market because there are so many stalls in one place, selling lots of different things.

Language features

In this Description, the following examples of language features (refer to pages 2–19) have been included:

language feature	*examples*
nouns	markets, cities, world, food, stalls, cheese, vegetables, toys, clothes, voices, shoppers, prices, lunch, snack, place, things
noun groups	dairy foods, meat and fish stalls, market days, market stall owners
adjectives	big, many, fresh, same, different, another, cheerful, some
present-tense relating verbs	are, has

>>

language feature	*examples*
present-tense action verbs	visit, sell, walk, call, stop
adverbs	always
prepositional phrases	in many cities, around the world, in the same place, for many years, in one part of the market, On market days, in cheerful voices, in one place

Sentences

The following sentence types (refer to pages 19–21) have also been included:

sentence type	*examples*
simple sentence	This market has hundreds of stalls. Meat and fish stalls are in a different area. Some shoppers stop to buy lunch or a snack.
complex sentence	There are also stalls that sell toys, clothes and lots of other goods. I always like to visit the market because there are so many stalls in one place, selling lots of different things.

Language effects

Some figurative language (refer to pages 26–31) may be suitable to add imagery to a description. Technical words and phrases (refer to page 31) related to a topic are included to provide accurate information for the reader. Evaluative language (refer to page 31) is generally included to express the author's opinion about the subject.

Vocabulary

When revising and editing a text, the writer can consider a more advanced or sophisticated choice of words (refer to pages 52–82).

In this text, the word *different* could be replaced with *separate*, and *buying* could be replaced with *purchasing*.

Text forms

A Description can be written in the form of:

- a blog
- a brochure or online advertisement
- a factual, fictional or character description
- a newspaper or magazine article
- an observation
- a spoken presentation.

Information Report

An Information Report is an informative text. The **purpose** of an Information Report is to present information that classifies living or non-living things.

Information Reports are generally written in present tense, unless the subject of the report no longer exists. In this instance, past tense can be used. An Information Report includes an evaluation that summarises the content and expresses the writer's thoughts about the subject.

The **audience** for an Information Report can vary, and may depend on the topic of the report. An Information Report about markets may appeal to families who visit the markets on the weekend; a report based on animal welfare may be written for a group of veterinary science students.

Text structure

Title

- The title names the subject of the report.

General statement

- The general statement identifies and classifies the subject.

Description

- The description provides information about the subject's physical appearance and other characteristics.
- The description is organised into paragraphs.
- Each paragraph begins with a topic sentence.
- Each paragraph includes supporting information that adds detail.

Evaluation

- The evaluation provides a summary statement about the subject. The writer's thoughts and attitude are usually expressed in the evaluation.

The following text models the appropriate structure for an Information Report.

Repurposed Recycling

In recent years, scientists have found ways to recycle and repurpose plastic items. This is important to prevent plastic from ending up in landfill, or from polluting our oceans and waterways. Scientists have been able to produce new and interesting goods from these discarded plastics.

One example is the recycling of plastic bottles and containers to make swimwear. The plastic items are shredded, melted and remade into yarn. This yarn can be skilfully woven into fabric that is suitable for swimwear. Another example is the recycling of plastic fishing nets. Discarded nets trap sea animals easily, causing many sea animals to drown.

Fishing nets also break down slowly in the ocean, releasing tiny pieces of plastic that can poison sea creatures and birds. To address these problems, discarded fishing nets are now being made into skateboards. The nets are shredded and melted down to form a type of plastic that is ideal to make a sturdy skateboard.

Products such as these demonstrate that plastic can be recycled and repurposed in clever ways. These types of leisure items can make our lives more enjoyable while keeping plastics from polluting the environment.

Language features

In this Information Report, the following examples of language features (refer to pages 2–19) have been included:

language feature	*examples*
nouns	scientists, landfill, oceans, waterways, example, plastics, swimwear, yarn, fabric, birds, problems, skateboards, environment
adjectives	recent, new, interesting, discarded, plastic, tiny, sturdy, clever, leisure
present-tense relating verbs	have, is, are
present-tense action verbs	trap, break down
adverbs	skilfully, easily, slowly
prepositional phrases	in recent years, in landfill, into yarn, for swimwear, in the ocean, in clever ways

Sentences

The following sentence types (refer to pages 19–21) have also been included:

sentence type	*examples*
simple sentence	Another example is the recycling of plastic fishing nets. Scientists have been able to produce new and interesting goods from these discarded plastics.

>>

sentence type	examples
complex sentence	Fishing nets also break down slowly in the ocean, releasing tiny pieces of plastic that can poison sea creatures and birds. The nets are shredded and melted down to form a type of plastic that is ideal to make a sturdy skateboard.

Language effects

Technical language (refer to page 31), or special words and phrases related to the topic, are used in Information Reports to provide accurate information for the reader. Evaluative language (refer to page 31) may be included to convey the writer's thoughts and attitudes to the reader.

Vocabulary

When revising and editing a text, the writer can consider a more advanced or sophisticated choice of words (refer to pages 52–82).

In this text, the word *important* could be replaced with *essential*, *problems* could be replaced with *issues*, and *clever* could be replaced with *innovative*.

Text forms

An Information Report can be written in the form of:

- a brochure
- a documentary
- a newspaper report
- a reference text
- a scientific, technological or social studies report
- a website.

Narrative

A Narrative is an imaginative text. The **purpose** of a Narrative is to entertain or instruct the reader by telling a series of events with a problem (complication) and a solution (resolution).

Narrative texts are written in past tense, although dialogue is written in present tense. A Narrative differs from a Recount in that it includes a problem that has to be solved by the characters in the story.

The **audience** for a Narrative text can be more generic, as the content is presented to entertain rather than instruct or inform. In a Narrative text, often the level of vocabulary and sentence structures determine who the appropriate audience will be.

Text structure

Title

- The title relates to the theme of the story.

Orientation

- The orientation introduces the main character in a setting of time and place.

Complication

- In the complication, the character encounters a problem.
- The complication, or plot, may involve more than one problem.
- Time and sequence words create a timeline for the events.
- The events are organised in paragraphs.
- Each paragraph begins with a topic sentence.
- Direct speech may be included.

Resolution

- The resolution explains how the problem was solved. Some narratives end with a moral or message. This is sometimes referred to as a coda.

The following text models the appropriate structure for a Narrative.

Minty Is Lost!

One evening, Sami and Dad came home from the shops.

Dad left the front door open as he carried in the shopping bags. Sami went to feed Minty, his pet rabbit.

But Minty's cage was empty. Sami searched all over the house. Minty was not there!

Dad helped Sami look outside for the little rabbit, but they couldn't find her. Minty was lost.

The next morning, Sami made colourful posters of Minty. Then, Sami and Dad put the posters up all along the street.

Later that day, Dad got a message on his phone. A lady had found Minty!

Sami and Dad rushed to the lady's house.

"I'm glad Minty is safe!" said Sami. Then, he gave Minty a big hug.

Language features

In this Narrative, the following examples of language features (refer to pages 2–19) have been included:

language feature	*examples*
nouns	house, rabbit, posters, street, message, hug
proper nouns	Sami, Dad, Minty
noun groups	front door, shopping bags, pet rabbit
adjectives	empty, colourful, big, little
past-tense verbs	was, came, carried, searched, helped, rushed
adverbs	outside
prepositional phrases	from the shops, for the little rabbit, on his phone, to the lady's house

Sentences

The following sentence types (refer to pages 19–21) have also been included:

sentence type	*examples*
simple sentence	Minty was lost. Sami went to feed Minty, his pet rabbit. The next day, Sami made colourful posters of Minty. A lady had found Minty!
compound sentence	Dad helped Sami look outside for the little rabbit, but they couldn't find her.
complex sentence	Dad left the front door open as he carried in the shopping bags.

Narrative Note

Questions, exclamations and direct speech are all typical features of narrative texts.

Language effects

Some figurative language, such as similes, metaphor, alliteration, idioms, onomatopoeia and personification (refer to pages 26–31), may be suitable to add imagery or humour to a narrative text.

Vocabulary

When revising and editing a text, the writer can consider a more advanced or sophisticated choice of words (refer to pages 52–82).

In this text, the word *got* could be replaced with *received,* and *said* could be replaced with *exclaimed.*

Text forms

A Narrative can be written in the form of:

- a film, television or audio script
- a folk tale, fairy tale, myth, legend or fable
- a novel or picture story book
- a play, poem or song
- a short story (adventure, fantasy, science fiction)
- a video or podcast script.

Procedure

A Procedure is an informative text. The **purpose** of a Procedure is to provide instructions about how to make or do something.

A Procedure includes the materials or equipment needed and the steps required to achieve the goal.

Procedural texts are written in present tense, because the instructions are telling the reader what to do next. Often, each step in the instructions for the Procedure begins with an action verb.

The **audience** for a procedural text can vary, and may depend on the topic of the Procedure. The instructions may be aimed at teaching students in a class how to play a game, or the instructions may include the steps to assemble a model car or knit a scarf.

Text structure

Title

- The title informs readers of what is going to be made or done.

Goal

- The goal outlines what is going to be achieved.
- The goal often begins with *To …* or *How to …*

Materials

- This section lists the materials needed to achieve the goal. Dot points are often used to create the list.
- The materials are listed in the order in which they occur in the steps.
- Other headings, such as *Ingredients* or *Equipment*, may be more appropriate.

Steps

- Other headings may be used such as *Method*, *Procedure* or *Instructions*.

>>

- Lists the steps in order of sequence.
- Numerals can be used to sequence the steps.
- Each step begins on a new line.
- Visual information may be included to clarify the Procedure.
- An experiment includes a summary of what was observed and a conclusion giving a final result.

The following text models the appropriate structure for a Procedure.

Making A Fruit Smoothie

Goal

To make and share a fruit smoothie

Ingredients

You will need:

- one small banana
- two cups of strawberries
- one cup of milk.

Steps

1. Peel the banana and place it into a blender.
2. Put the strawberries into the blender with the banana.
3. Pour the milk slowly into the blender.
4. Place the lid firmly on the blender. Blend the fruit and milk together.
5. Remove the lid. Pour the smoothie into two glasses.
6. Share your healthy fruit smoothie with a friend!

Language features

In this Procedure, the following examples of language features (refer to pages 2–19) have been included:

language feature	***examples***
nouns	banana, blender, strawberries, milk, glasses
noun groups	fruit smoothie
adjectives	small, healthy
present-tense action verbs	peel, put, pour, place, blend, remove, share
adverbs	slowly, firmly, together
prepositional phrases	into a blender, into two glasses, with a friend

Sentences

The following sentence types (refer to pages 19–21) have also been included:

sentence type	***examples***
simple sentence	Remove the lid.
compound sentence	Peel the banana and place it into a blender.

Procedure Note

Steps in a Procedure are usually numbered. They generally begin with a present-tense verb (command) to instruct the reader how to complete each step. Steps in more complex procedures may begin with an adverb, or an adverbial phrase or clause.

Language effects

Technical language (refer to page 31) can be used in procedural texts.

Vocabulary

When revising and editing a text, the writer can consider a more advanced or sophisticated choice of words (refer to pages 52–82).

In this text, the word *slowly* could be replaced with *carefully*, and *healthy* could be replaced with *delicious*.

Text forms

A Procedure can be written in the form of:

- directions to get to a particular place
- an instruction manual
- a recipe
- instructions for a game or how to make something
- a science experiment
- a timetable.

Exposition

An Exposition is a persuasive text. The **purpose** of an Exposition is to persuade readers by arguing one side of an issue.

Exposition texts are written in present tense, because the writer is persuading the reader to agree with the arguments being presented. The Exposition begins with a statement explaining the writer's opinion and is followed by the arguments supporting this point of view.

The **audience** for an Exposition text can vary, and may depend on the topic being argued. The arguments being presented may be directed at a parent, a teacher at school or a member of a particular community group.

Text structure

Title

- The title informs readers of the issue that is going to be argued.

Statement of position

- The statement of position explains the writer's point of view and previews the arguments.

Series of arguments

- Each argument is described and listed in order of importance.
- The arguments are organised in paragraphs.
- Time and sequence words may be used to arrange the arguments.
- Each paragraph includes supporting information or evidence.

Concluding statement

- The concluding statement reinforces the statement of position to persuade readers. Often, a solution or possible action is suggested.

The following text models the appropriate structure for an Exposition.

Browndale Primary School Assembly
Monday, 14 March

Bike Safety Rules Are Important

I think it is very important to follow bike safety rules when you are riding your bike.

First, wear a bike helmet. It will protect your head if you have an accident. You should wear brightly coloured clothes, too, so car drivers can easily see you.

Second, always ride on a bike path or in a bike lane if you can. These are much safer places to ride because cars do not go on them.

Last, I feel it is important to learn the road rules and follow the road signs.

If everyone does this, the roads will be much safer places for bike riders.

By following bike safety rules, I believe you will all stay safe and have fun riding your bikes.

Thank you,

Amelia

Language features

In this Exposition, the following examples of language features (refer to pages 2–19) have been included:

language feature	*examples*
nouns	bike, clothes, cars, roads
noun groups	bike safety rules, bike helmet, car drivers

>>

language feature	*examples*
adjectives	coloured, safer
present-tense verbs	follow, protect, wear, see, ride, learn, stay
sensing verbs	think, feel, believe
adverbs	easily, always
time and sequence words	first, second, last
prepositional phrases	on a bike path, for bike riders

Sentences

The following sentence types (refer to pages 19–21) have also been included:

sentence type	*examples*
simple sentence	First, wear a bike helmet.
compound sentence	You should wear brightly coloured clothes, too, so car drivers can easily see you.
complex sentence	It will protect your head if you have an accident.

Exposition Note

In an Exposition, the most important argument is written first.

Language effects

Persuasive language (refer to page 31) is used in Exposition texts, to persuade the reader to agree with the arguments presented.

Vocabulary

When revising and editing a text, the writer can consider a more advanced or sophisticated choice of words (refer to pages 52–82).

In this text, the word *go* could be replaced with *travel*, and *important* could be replaced with *essential*.

Text forms

An Exposition can be written in the form of:

- an advertisement
- an essay
- a flyer or leaflet
- a letter or speech
- a newspaper, newsletter or magazine article
- a podcast
- social media posts.

Explanation

An Explanation is an informative text. The **purpose** of an Explanation is to explain how or why something occurs.

Explanation texts are written in present tense, because the text explains a sequence of events that occurs based on time or cause. Titles of explanation texts sometimes begin with the words *How* or *Why* and often explore scientific themes or topics.

The **audience** for an explanation text can vary, and may depend on the topic of the Explanation. The text may be written in response to a person asking a question, or it may explain a scientific phenomenon to a much wider audience.

Text structure

Title

- The title informs readers what the Explanation is going to be about. The title sometimes begins with *How* … or *Why* …

Identifying statement

- The identifying statement tells what is to be explained.
- This first paragraph may include some background information about the topic.

Explanation sequence

- This part of the text explains a series of events or cause and effect.
- Events are linked by time or by cause and effect.
- Information about the events is grouped in paragraphs.
- Each paragraph begins with a topic sentence.
- Each paragraph includes supporting detail about *how* or *why*.

Summary statement

- The final statement draws all the information together.

The following text models the appropriate structure for an Explanation.

The Life Cycle of a Stick Insect

The life cycle of a stick insect has three stages. These are the egg, the nymph and the adult stick insect.

During autumn, a female stick insect lays her eggs from up in a tree. One at a time, the eggs drop onto the ground among the leaves.

In spring, the eggs hatch and tiny nymphs come out. A nymph looks like an adult stick insect, but much smaller.

The nymph sheds its skin. Then, it quickly climbs up onto a plant or tree, because it needs to find new leaves to eat.

During the next three months, the nymph sheds its skin four more times. Each time, the nymph grows bigger. Finally, the nymph becomes an adult stick insect. Then, an adult female lays new eggs and the life cycle starts again.

Language features

In this Explanation, the following examples of language features (refer to pages 2–19) have been included:

language feature	*examples*
nouns	stages, autumn, eggs, tree, ground, leaves, nymph, spring
noun groups	life cycle, stick insect, adult stick insect, adult female
adjectives	tiny, smaller, new, next, bigger
present-tense relating verbs	has, are

>>

language feature	*examples*
present-tense action verbs	lays, drop, hatch, sheds, climbs, grows, becomes, starts
adverbs	quickly, again, up, then, finally
prepositional phrases	in a tree, onto the ground, among the leaves, onto a plant or tree

Sentences

The following sentence types (refer to pages 19–21) have also been included:

sentence type	*examples*
simple sentence	The life cycle of a stick insect has three stages.
compound sentence	In spring, the eggs hatch and tiny nymphs come out.
complex sentence	Then, it quickly climbs up onto a plant or tree, because it needs to find new leaves to eat.

Note that some sentences show cause and effect, e.g. *Then, it quickly climbs up onto a plant or tree, because it needs to find new leaves to eat.*

Language effects

Technical language (refer to page 31), or special words and phrases related to the topic, are used in explanation texts to provide accurate information for the reader.

Vocabulary

When revising and editing a text, the writer can consider a more advanced or sophisticated choice of words (refer to pages 52–82).

In this text, the word *has* could be replaced with *consists of*, and *starts again* could be replaced with *is repeated*.

Text forms

An Explanation can be written in the form of:

- a spoken presentation or interview
- a brochure, newspaper article or podcast
- a flow chart
- an essay
- a magazine article or website.

Discussion

A Discussion is a persuasive text. The **purpose** of a Discussion is to examine more than one side of an issue.

Discussion texts are written in present tense, because the arguments are being presented to persuade the reader to agree with the writer. A Discussion outlines the issue being discussed and presents arguments 'for' and 'against' the topic.

The **audience** for a discussion text can vary, and may depend on the topic of the discussion. A Discussion about a school-based issue could be presented to students at a school assembly, or a community issue could be discussed in the local newspaper.

Text structure

Title

- The title identifies the issue that is going to be discussed.

Opening statement

- The opening statement outlines the issue. It may also include some background information about the topic.

Arguments 'for' and 'against'

- The arguments include evidence in support of and against the issue.
- The arguments are organised in paragraphs, with the most important argument first.
- The arguments *for* the issue are usually written first.
- Time and sequence words are often used to arrange the arguments.
- Each paragraph begins with a topic sentence, followed by supporting information.
- Text connectives are usually used when there is a change of argument.

Concluding statement

- The final statement is a summary of the issue and the writer's opinion.

The following text models the appropriate structure for a Discussion.

Is it Better to Drum or Strum?

Many people enjoy playing a musical instrument. My brother, Dan, plays the guitar, but I would much rather play the drums!

Firstly, drums are suitable for anyone wanting to play a musical instrument. You can easily practise keeping the beat by tapping along with the drumsticks and pedals to your favourite music.

Also, research indicates that playing the drums is an excellent way to improve coordination. As you learn more complex rhythms, your brain works harder to control the fine, rapid movements of your hands and feet while playing. This requires a lot of practice, but it's so satisfying when you get it right!

However, Dan doesn't like playing the drums. He prefers the guitar because it provides an outlet for his creativity. He enjoys the contrast of plucking individual strings to produce soft sounds with strumming multiple strings to make loud, harmonious chords.

He also likes getting together with his friends to play music, and the guitar is more convenient than drums because it is portable.

Throughout the world, music has the unique ability to unite people. Ultimately, it doesn't matter which instrument you play, but I'd definitely prefer to drum than to strum!

Language features

In this Discussion, the following examples of language features (refer to pages 2–19) have been included:

language feature	*examples*
nouns	people, guitar, drums, beat, drumsticks, pedals, brain, practice, contrast, ability
proper nouns	Dan

>>

language feature	*examples*
noun groups	musical instrument, soft sounds
adjectives	suitable, favourite, excellent, complex, fine, rapid, satisfying, individual, multiple, loud, harmonious, convenient, portable, unique
present-tense action verbs	indicates, learn, works, requires
sensing verbs	enjoys, prefers, likes
modal verbs	would (... play), can (... practise)
adverbs	Firstly, easily, along, harder, so, also, together, Ultimately, definitely
conjunctions	but, because, and

Sentences

The following sentence types (refer to pages 19–21) have also been included:

sentence type	*examples*
simple sentence	Many people enjoy playing a musical instrument. However, Dan doesn't like playing the drums. He enjoys the contrast of plucking individual strings to produce soft sounds with strumming multiple strings to make loud, harmonious chords.
compound sentence	My brother, Dan, plays the guitar, but I would much rather play the drums!
complex sentence	As you learn more complex rhythms, your brain works harder to control the fine, rapid movements of your hands and feet while playing. He prefers the guitar because it provides an outlet for his creativity.

Discussion Note

Reported speech is sometimes used in the writing of discussion texts.

Language effects

Persuasive language (refer to page 31) is used in discussion texts, to persuade the reader to agree with the arguments presented by the writer.

Vocabulary

When revising and editing a text, the writer can consider a more advanced or sophisticated choice of words (refer to pages 52–82).

In this text, the words *a lot of* could be replaced with *regular*, and *harmonious* could be replaced with *blended*.

Text forms

A Discussion can be written in the form of:

- a lecture
- a newspaper, newsletter or magazine opinion piece
- podcast
- a radio segment script
- a speech or debate.

Response

A Response is an informative text. The **purpose** of a Response is to give an opinion about a written or visual work, object or event.

Response texts are often written in present tense, but can be written in past tense if the subject of the Response is a work or object that no longer exists, or is an event that has taken place. The Response concludes with a judgement by the writer about the subject.

The **audience** for a Response text can vary, and may depend on the topic of the Response. A Response to a music concert may be shared with peers, or a Response to visiting an art gallery may be shared with the art teacher at school.

Text structure

Title

- The title informs readers of the subject of the Response.

Context

- The opening paragraph states information about the work, object or event.
- This part of the text sometimes previews the writer's opinion or provides background information about the subject.

Description

- The description provides information about the features of the work, object or event.
- Each paragraph introduces a different aspect of the subject.
- Each paragraph begins with a topic sentence.
- Each paragraph includes information that supports the writer's opinion.

Judgement

- The final statement gives the writer's opinion based on the description.

The following text models the appropriate structure for a Response.

The Hidden Dinosaur Forest

The Hidden Dinosaur Forest is an exciting book about a girl who finds some living dinosaurs.

The main character is Cassie. She is eight years old. Cassie goes on a special trip with her grandparents. They are scientists who look for dinosaur fossils.

Cassie and her grandparents crawl through a gap in a cave. They are very surprised to find a hidden forest, full of dinosaurs!

My favourite part of the story is when a baby triceratops suddenly hatches from an egg. It thinks Cassie is its mother. But this gets dangerous for Cassie!

The pictures are beautiful. There is a map, too. It shows the places where events in the story happen.

I think that children who like dinosaurs will really love this book!

Language features

In this Response, the following examples of language features (refer to pages 2–19) have been included:

language feature	*examples*
nouns	dinosaurs, grandparents, scientists
proper nouns	*The Hidden Dinosaur Forest*, Cassie
noun groups	dinosaur fossils, baby triceratops
adjectives	living, hidden, favourite, dangerous
present-tense relating verbs	is, are
present-tense action verbs	finds, goes, crawl, hatches, shows

>>

language feature	*examples*
sensing verbs	think, like, love
adverbs	suddenly, really
prepositional phrases	on a special trip, through a gap

Sentences

The following sentence types (refer to pages 19–21) have also been included:

sentence type	*examples*
simple sentence	The main character is Cassie. Cassie goes on a special trip with her grandparents. But this gets dangerous for Cassie!
complex sentence	They are scientists who look for dinosaur fossils. It shows the places where events in the story happen.

Language effects

Some figurative language (refer to pages 26–31), such as similes, can be used in response texts to add imagery.

Persuasive language (refer to page 31) may also be included to encourage the reader to agree with the writer's judgement.

Vocabulary

When revising and editing a text, the writer can consider a more advanced or sophisticated choice of words (refer to pages 52–82).

In this text, the word *special* could be replaced with *amazing*, and *very surprised* could be replaced with *astonished*.

Text forms

A Response can be written in the form of:

- a book review
- a film, video or documentary review
- a newspaper or newsletter article
- a personal response
- a restaurant review
- social media comments.

Hybrid Text

A Hybrid text can take two distinct forms: a blended text where two or more different text types are combined into one, or a dual text about the same topic written using two or more text types. Many Hybrid texts combine a Narrative with a factual text type, and frequently one text type is more dominant that the other.

Each text type within the blended Hybrid text retains some of the typical structural features and many of the language features of the individual text type.

The placement of the individual text types within the Hybrid text can differ, thus the overall structure of a Hybrid text has many variations.

The **purpose** of a Hybrid text is determined by the chosen text types that are included. There is likely to be more than one purpose due to the combination of text types within the Hybrid text.

The **audience** for a Hybrid text also depends on the combination of text types presented by the writer. A text may include a humorous Narrative about an incident with a dog, combined with an Exposition that argues that dogs are better pets than cats. This Hybrid could be used by a child to persuade parents to allow the child to have a dog for a pet.

The following text models an appropriate structure for a Hybrid text: a Recount written in first person; and an Information Report about petrichor, the smell of rain. (The Information Report is indicated with a dotted underline.)

This text uses a common A–B–A structure, where Part A represents the sections of recounted text and Part B represents an Information Report based on facts about petrichor.

Hybrid texts typically showcase an extensive range of language features, as they portray the complex vocabulary and figurative language of fiction texts in combination with the technical language of factual texts.

Petrichor Perfume

It had been several years since I'd heard the drumming of raindrops on our roof. My parents were stressed; the land was as dry as a bone, and they couldn't see a light at the end of the tunnel. Reportedly, this was the harshest drought in over seven decades.

After dinner, I lay on my bed, listening to a podcast. I really needed a distraction – something that would transport me away from parched paddocks.

"In today's podcast," began Dr Barberis, "I will be discussing the smell of rain! That's right – rain really does have a scent! This specific aroma is known as *petrichor*, a Greek word meaning 'stone' and 'fluid'.

"During dry periods, a yellowish plant oil accumulates in the soil. When the air is humid, the pores of stones, rocks and soil fill with tiny amounts of water. This water releases the smell of the plant oil, which has the unique *petrichor* perfume. When the rain falls and the soil is disturbed, this scent becomes even stronger ..."

When the podcast had finished, I walked outside onto the verandah. I instinctively sniffed the night air. Was I imagining that smell? Perhaps, after hearing the podcast, I was just imagining the earthy fragrance?

But then, I saw a flash of lightning dance across the sky. A gentle pitter-patter on the roof was soon a booming symphony of sounds. I realised I wasn't dreaming!

Dad walked outside to join me. A huge smile replaced the deep lines of worry and fatigue on his face and my overwhelming sense of despair washed away.

Petrichor had delivered.

Language features

In this Hybrid text, the following examples of language features (refer to pages 2–19) have been included:

language feature	***examples***
nouns	decades, podcast, distraction, pores, fatigue
proper nouns	Dr Barberis, Greek, Dad
noun groups	Greek word, yellowish plant oil, unique *petrichor* perfume
adjectives	several, parched, humid, booming, overwhelming
past-tense verbs	heard, were stressed, had finished, walked, sniffed, realised, replaced, had delivered
present-tense verbs	does, accumulates, releases, becomes
adverbs	really, quickly, away
time and sequence words	after dinner, when the podcast had finished
prepositional phrases	in the soil, onto the verandah, across the sky

Sentences

The following sentence types (refer to pages 19–21) have also been included:

sentence type	***examples***
simple sentence	I realised I wasn't dreaming! Dad walked outside to join me.

>>

sentence type	*examples*
compound sentence	A huge smile replaced the deep lines of worry and fatigue on his face and my overwhelming sense of despair washed away.
complex sentence	When the podcast had finished, I walked outside onto the verandah.

Language effects

The language effects (refer to pages 25–31) suitable for Hybrid texts depend on the text types included in the text. Refer to the language features section of specific text types.

These language effects have been included:

language effect	*examples*
alliteration	parched paddocks, symphony of sounds
idiom	a light at the end of the tunnel
metaphor	lightning danced across the sky
personification	Petrichor had delivered
simile	as dry as a bone

Poetry

Poetry is a form of personal expression. Writers may respond to a situation, retell an adventure or describe an object, event or experience. In poetry, a variety of different language features is used, particularly nouns and adjectives. They are supported by the use of figurative language, which creates vivid imagery.

Writers can choose any structure for their poem, but there are some recognised types of poems with specific characteristics. Some of the most common types of poetry are listed below.

Acrostic

An acrostic poem uses certain letters, most often the first letter in each line, to form a word or message when read vertically.

Poems

Poetry is creative
One way of expressing
Emotive, imaginative or descriptive thoughts.
There is a world of scope for
Rhyme, rhythm and rhetoric.
You, the writer, have a blank page.

Ballad

A ballad tells a story, often with a theme of sadness, adventure or heroism.

Characteristics of ballads are:

- short verses of four lines
- an A–B–C–B rhyming pattern (meaning the last word in the second and fourth lines should rhyme)
- a definite rhythm of alternating strong and weak beats (iambic foot).

Poetry Note

Many poems have a rhythm. Iambic foot is the natural rhythm or pattern in spoken English made by the weak or strong beat given to the syllables in words.

Iambic foot is most evident in song lyrics and poetry. Read the following extract from "Our Holiday" out loud to discover the iambic foot.

I **squeezed** my **things** in**side** the **car**,
And **just** to **name** a **few**,
I **had** a **buck**et, **spade** and **surf**board
And the **beach** um**brel**la **too!**

Chant

A chant is a verse or short piece of text that can be sung, read or spoken, usually by more than one person.

Our School

All of us are children from the Bay Street Primary School,
We always work together and we follow every rule,
Sometimes we're in sporting teams, and sometimes we debate,
But we always wear our uniform to walk in through the gate.

Cinquain

A cinquain is a poem with five lines, each with a specific purpose.

A common structure for a cinquain is: Line 1 has one word (the title). Line 2 describes the title, and may include adjectives. Line 3 describes actions of the subject, using one or more verbs. Line 4 expresses a feeling. Line 5 has one or two words that recall the title.

Lions

Lions,
Majestic cats,
Stalking through the grasses,
Top of the animal hierarchy,
Jungle royalty.

Free verse

Free verse is written in either rhymed or unrhymed lines that have no fixed rhythm pattern.

Thunder booming and raindrops drumming,
Like percussion instruments in an orchestra.

Haiku

Haiku is a style of poetry that comes from Japan. Haiku are composed of three unrhymed lines of five, seven and five syllables. Themes are usually associated with nature.

Rainbow

Seven coloured bands,
Reaching out across the sky,
Towards the treasure.

Limerick

A limerick is a short, funny poem consisting of five lines. Characteristics of limericks are:

- Lines 1, 2 and 5 have the same rhythm; lines 3 and 4 have the same rhythm, with fewer syllables than the other lines
- A–A–B–B–A rhyming pattern (meaning lines 1, 2 and 5 rhyme, and lines 3 and 4 rhyme)
- Words are often shortened or altered, to maintain either the rhythm or rhyming patterns.

There was an old lady called Pip,
Who wanted to do a road trip,
But her children said, "No!
Your driving's too slow!"
So they booked her a cruise on a ship.

Narrative

A narrative poem tells a story. It is similar in structure to a narrative text, with an orientation, complication and a resolution. There are no fixed line lengths or rhyme patterns.

From "The Dream"

If you wake up with a fright
In the middle of the night,
It's likely that you've had a scary dream.
There could be hairy monsters chasing you,
Or much worse still, embracing you,
But things may not be quite the way they seem.

Quatrain

A quatrain consists of four lines. A common structure for a quatrain is: Lines 2 and 4 must rhyme and generally contain a similar number of syllables to maintain the rhythm and flow of the language. Lines 1 and 3 can rhyme, but do not have to.

Blossoms

The blossoms are so beautiful,
They decorate the trees,
So appealing to the insects,
But they only make me sneeze.

Rhyme

A rhyming poem is a general term for a poem that has the repetition of the same or similar sounds at the end of alternate lines or each pair of lines.

My New Bike

I have a classy brand-new bike,
It's sparkly red, which I quite like,
I ride it every day to school,
My friends all think it's really cool!

Writing Checklist

Students can use this checklist to assist them with the planning, drafting, revising, editing and publishing stages of their writing.

The purpose of the text is ______________________________

____

____

The audience for the text is ______________________________

____

____

The text type is ______________________________

____

The title of the text is ______________________________

____

The sections of the text structure are:

- ______________________________
- ______________________________
- ______________________________
- ______________________________

I have used:

☐ past-tense verbs

☐ present-tense verbs

I have used:

☐ simple sentences

☐ compound sentences

☐ complex sentences

I have included these language features:

- [ ] nouns and pronouns
- [ ] adjectives
- [ ] relating verbs
- [ ] action verbs
- [ ] adverbs
- [ ] time and sequence words/phrases
- [ ] conjunctions and connectives
- [ ] phrases (prepositional/adverbial/adjectival)

I have used:

- [ ] technical language
- [ ] evaluative language
- [ ] figurative language

I have:

- [ ] used correct punctuation in the text
- [ ] used rich vocabulary in the text
- [ ] checked the spelling of unfamiliar words in the text
- [ ] revised and edited the text prior to publication.

Index

Bold page references show the main reference for entries with several references.

Q

R